SAVORING ITALY

SAVORING ITALY

Photographs by Robert Freson

Edited by Alexandra Arrowsmith

*Essays by Carol Field, Leslie Forbes, Barbara Grizzuti Harrison,
Louis Inturrisi, Beatrice Muzi, Paola Pettini, Vito Quaranta, Nadia Stancioff,
Sam Tanenhaus, and Vanessa Somers Vreeland*

Recipes gathered in Italy by Marilyn Costa

HarperCollins*Publishers*

Callaway Editions
1992

FIRST EDITION

Library of Congress Cataloging-in-Publication Data

Savoring Italy / photographs by Robert Freson;
essays by Carol Field . . . [et al.];
recipes gathered in Italy by Marilyn Costa.
p. cm.
Includes index.
ISBN 0-06-016900-1
1. Cookery, Italian. 2. Italy — Social life and customs.
I. Freson, Robert. II. Field, Carol. III. Costa, Marilyn.
TX723.S343 1992   92-52584
641.5945–dc20

92 93 94 95 96   10 9 8 7 6 5 4 3 2 1

CONTENTS

VALLE
D'AOSTA
II

• Aosta

L. Maggiore

L. Como

ALTO
ADIGE
I

• Bolzano

Adige

• Tolmezzo

FRIULI
I

• Udine

PIEDMONT
II

LOMBARDY
III

• Milan

• Maleo

• Verona

VENETO
I

Piave

• Trieste

Turin •

Po

L. Garda

Po

• Mantua

Po

• Venice

Roddi •   • Alba

• Parma

• Reggio
nell'Emilia

• Rubiera   • Modena

EMILIA-
ROMAGNA
V

• Bologna

• Genoa

Recco •   • Portofino

LIGURIA
II

• Ravenna

Lucca •

• Fiesole

• Florence

Arno

Pisa •

Ligurian Sea

TUSCANY
IV

• Siena

L. *Trasimeno*

• Ancona

LE
MARCHE
VI

Sinalunga •

• Perugia
• Assisi

• Montepulciano

UMBRIA VI

• Todi

• Norcia

L. Bolsena

• Orvieto

Adriatic Sea

• Viterbo

L. Bracciano

• Pescara

• L'Aquila

Tiber

ABRUZZI
VII

• Rome

LAZIO
VI

MOLISE
VII

GARGANO
MASSIF

Liri

Volturno

SARDINIA
IX

Nuoro •

CAMPANIA
VII

APULIA
VIII

• Bari

TRULLI
DISTRICT

• Naples

• Potenza

• Alberobello

• Amalfi

• Matera

• Brindisi

BASILICATA
VIII

• Taranto

Tyrrhenian Sea

• Cagliari

• Castrovillari

CALABRIA
VII

• Cosenza

• Catanzaro

Ionian Sea

• Palermo

• Taormina

SICILY
IX

Mediterranean Sea

• Agrigento

Introduction

IN 1983 I HAD THE PLEASURE of publishing *The Taste of France,* a book exploring the regional foods of that country. Subsequently, with the generous help of the *London Sunday Times Magazine,* I was able to turn my attention to Italy, France's sister country in gastronomy.

I wanted to record, while it was still possible, the relationship between regional resources, climate, produce, and people, and the richness of recipes created in each part of Italy. I had discovered earlier, in France, an intriguing rapport between the elements of each region, the soil, the people, and the ways the people adapted the locally available ingredients (what could be grown, raised, fished, or hunted nearby) into the most palatable dishes.

This resourcefulness grew out of necessity in both countries, of course, from the lack of communication between regions as well as the lack of advanced methods of food preservation. But as its economy grew more prosperous and mobile, Italy would become more homogeneous, and the pleasures of experiencing a great diversity of regional dishes as you travel from north to south or from the Adriatic to the Mediterranean would be dissipated by the modern advantages of refrigeration and a vastly improved system of transportation.

Luckily, this uniformity of cuisine in Italy is balanced today by a significant rebirth of interest in the very refined specialties that were originally available only near their place of creation. All kinds of fresh fish and shellfish, meat, game, fruits, cheeses, and preserved meats now move easily all over the country, but happily, during my whole year of searching through all corners of Italy, we discovered many chefs and restaurants who pride themselves on preserving their regional integrity. They helped us immensely by revealing their old family recipes and by letting me photograph different stages in the preparation of local specialties. Without them I could not have put this book together, and throughout the pages describing each region I will credit them for their knowledge and contribution.

I am grateful to all of the writers who have shared here their love and remembrances of Italy, its cuisine and character. Vito Quaranta and Paola Pettini not only penned thoughtful writings about their homelands, but also influenced the foods we chose to photograph in their regions. I only wish that Carol Field, Leslie Forbes, Barbara Grizzuti Harrison, Louis Inturrisi, Beatrice Muzi, Nadia Stancioff, Sam Tanenhaus, and Vanessa Somers Vreeland could have been along with us on our journeys as well. Nevertheless, I appreciate their help in capturing the spirit of this country.

Even though I encountered many changes due to the modernization of food production, the natural beauty and richness of Italy and its historical heritage have not altered where they are essential and expected. Local markets still reflect the originality of regional products, just as the beautiful faces of the people who make them reflect pride in their accomplishments.

It is to them that I dedicate this book.

Robert Freson

A typical small grocery shop front in Venice in the 1950s.

◄ OVERLEAF
*The famous gondolas of Venice lined up in front of the Doges' Palace, with
the Piazza San Marco to the right. The Church of Santa Maria della Salute
heralds the entrance to the Grand Canal in the background.*

I. *Veneto / Alto Adige / Friuli*

W<small>E HAVE LIVED IN THE VENETO</small> for more than thirty years, and the region continues to fascinate and amaze us. Industrialization has, of course, introduced cement to the countryside, and massive tourism has led to extreme overcrowding. Nonetheless, the gently rolling hills, elegant mountains, lagoons, and even the flats with their winter mists make for an intimate, suggestive region in which sea, plain, and mountain succeed one another in pleasing rhythm.

Like the countryside, the dialect of the Veneto population is a gentle one. It is easy to find oneself chatting in the yards of rural homes; in village inns; in the old quarters of the cities, while enjoying a "shadow," or glass, of white wine; in the fish and vegetable markets in the piazzas; or while walking along the narrow streets. This gentleness, perhaps the real soul of the Veneto, is not the result of a lack of virility but rather the fruit of years of civilization.

The civilization of the Veneto is ancient indeed. The first settlements of pre–Indo-European people were displaced in the tenth century B.C. by the Venetians, who had originated in the Balkans and who brought Iron Age civilization with them. In the mid-third century B.C., the Romans moved into the area. After a period of prosperity and well-being, which saw, during the first three centuries of the Christian era, the growth of the region's cities, a period of slow decline began in the fourth century.

This decline, precipitated by the struggle between the Goths and the Byzantines, culminated in the fifth century in the barbarian invasions. At this time, the Venetians, fleeing the invaders, abandoned the mainland for the islands, later founding the city of Venice. With the mainland in the hands of the Longobards and with the maritime territory under Byzantine domination, the Venetian Republic began to grow, imposing its dominion on the seas and gradually conquering the mainland towns.

While the preparation of food in the Veneto was simple under the Longobards, the Byzantines introduced new, decisive flavors: onion, garlic, and hot pepper. The cuisine reached maximum refinement under the Venetian Republic, which imported Oriental spices (pepper, cinnamon, cloves) to enrich the numerous courses of game and fish, plentiful in the lagoon and the delta of the Po River. After the fall of Venice, the Veneto came to be ruled by the Austro-Hungarian empire and was thus exposed to the influences of Austrian and German cooking.

The regional cuisine of the Veneto as we know it today began to take shape around the turn of the twentieth century, and has come to occupy a prominent place in Italian gastronomy. To understand its nuances, one must understand the land from which it comes. The territory of the Veneto includes a number of different natural regions. The most stunning and varied of these is the Alps, a series of high plateaux from which mountain ranges of powerful, elegant beauty emerge, while the pre-Alpine region of small hills is softer and gentler. This mountainous territory provides grazing for sheep and goats—from whose milk excellent cheeses and ricotta are made—as well as reindeer and hare. The cone-shaped Euganean and Berician Hills which arise between the Alps and the plain have their own unique ecosystem. This area is renowned for its exquisite *prosciutti.* The vast plain of the Veneto consists in part of lagoon, and in part of the coastal region that extends from the delta of the Po to the Tagliamento River, and then to the Padana plain. The coastal and lagoon regions boast an abundance of fish, shellfish, and other seafood. The delta of the Adige River has an infinite variety of vegetables and aquatic game, bass, eel, and red mullet; the plain is the region of cattle, hogs, and poultry. With all this diversity the Veneto has managed to maintain a strong agricultural and food industry despite the industrialization of the last thirty years, somewhat in contrast to other parts of Italy.

High quality and great variety distinguish the cooking of this region. Polenta is the thread that ties together the cuisine of the seven provinces into which the Veneto is divided (recipe page 25). A mixture of ground meal and water, polenta constituted the main staple of the Veneto peasant's diet for centuries, particularly during periods of famine or pestilence. At first, polenta was made from fava beans, chickpeas, and millet; later, it was made from corn, which initially was imported by the Venetians, who then began to cultivate it in the Po delta. Traditionally, polenta was prepared in a pot filled with water and hung above a flame; the cook poured the ground corn into the pot and, after adding salt, stirred the mixture with a wooden spoon, gradually increasing the force as the polenta thickened. Once the desired consistency had been reached, the polenta was poured steaming onto a wooden cutting board, where it was cut into large strips. Polenta, which appears in many traditional dishes of the Veneto, currently is enjoying a culinary revival.

Any gastronomic itinerary of this region must center on Venice. The city marries a seafood-based cuisine—both simple and sumptuous, due to the perfection and freshness of the ingredients—to a cuisine tied to the products of the countryside and enlivened by spices and herbs that evoke the city's commercial past. We have dishes such as *broeto* (a fish soup), fish *in saor* (fried and covered with a sweet-and-sour sauce made with fried onions, sugar, vinegar, and raisins), and *grancevola alla veneziana* (boiled crab served in the shell and seasoned with oil, lemon juice, and parsley). Another specialty is *fegato alla veneziana* (calf's liver cut into thin strips and cooked in oil, butter, and onion), whose essential character lies in the harmonic balance between the flavors of liver and onion (recipe page 29). *Risi e bisi* (rice with peas cooked in broth) is but one version of *risotto,* a creamy rice dish made throughout the Veneto. *Baccalà* (codfish) and *stoccafisso* (dried cod) are common in other provinces.

One cannot appreciate the food of Venice completely without knowing its inhabitants, whose most salient characteristic is conviviality. Any occasion justifies a trip to the *osteria* to chat with friends, glass of wine in hand, and to snack on various appetizers, such as hard-boiled eggs and fresh red radishes. People also visit the *osteria* on their way home in the evening, to discuss the events of the day in the gentle local dialect. The city's soul is best revealed, however, during the traditional holidays. In centuries past, the year was filled with a great number of feast days created to celebrate a wide spectrum of historic and religious events. The most renowned of these was the wedding of the sea, which symbolized Venice's dominant role in the Adriatic. This celebration culminated in the speech of the Doge, who, having arrived in a richly

A woman cleaning peppers by wiping them with a dry towel in Ronchi di Castelnuovo in the Veneto.

Peperoni sofritti, *peppers cooked with olive oil, at the home of Mr. Quaranta in Ronchi di Castelnuovo.*

OPPOSITE▶

Lumache alle erbette, *also called* bogoni alle erbe, *snails cooked with vegetables, here at Mr. Quaranta's home in Ronchi di Castelnuovo.*

A fruit stand at the Rialto market in Venice.

adorned boat (the famous *Bucintoro*), threw a wedding ring into the sea, saying, "Under the sign of eternal dominion, we, the Doge of Venice, now wed thee, O sea." Even today, Venetians are devoted to these festivals, especially *Carnevale,* when revelers sport masks in the most varied styles. Desserts commonly eaten on these occasions include *zaleti,* flattened, oval biscuits made with flour, butter, eggs, spices, and raisins; *baicoli,* wonderful cookies eaten with chocolate or *zabaione; fritole,* made from flour, raisins, pine nuts, candied lime, and sugar; and *galani,* fried pastries typical of the carnival season.

Padua, home of the first universities, is known for its poultry, which at one time was raised by women on farms and, to a greater extent, on country estates, although large-scale farming has taken over now. Geese, capons, guinea fowl, pigeons, roosters, hens, and ducks are mainstays of Paduan cooking. Verona, best known for the opera performances in its Roman amphitheater, celebrates carnival season with gastronomic festivities. Near the border of the province of Mantua, squash *tortellini* are a specialty (recipe page 22), while in the countryside, cooked snails with fresh herbs are favorites, as are preserved peaches. In the area around Vicenza, noted for the exquisite asparagus of Bassano, *toresan* (pigeon in the local dialect) or other poultry, skewered and roasted, is popular. A typical dish here is *baccalà alla vicentina,* slices of dried, salt-cured codfish stuffed with onion, garlic, parsley, anchovies, and grated Parmigiano, braised in a pan with a sauce of milk and olive oil.

The Treviso area is famous for its landscape and for the patrician villages that appear suddenly between rows of vineyards and splendid Italian-style gardens. Built in centuries past by wealthy Venetian merchants who competed for the services of the most famous architects and painters of interiors, these villas were not only vacation homes but also the centers of vast agricultural estates. Typical products of the area are radicchio, for which a fair is held in Castelfranco Veneto during the week before Christmas, and the mushrooms of Montello. The region around Belluno is known for its beans, especially the Lamon variety, first introduced to this region in the 1500s from Central America. These beans are the main ingredient in the popular *pasta e fagioli,* pasta and bean soup (recipe page 28), and in other flavorful soups. Also typical are *casonzei* (*ravioli* stuffed with spinach and *prosciutto*), *risotto* with snails, and numerous game dishes. Finally, in the province of Rovigo, we find a simpler cuisine. Fish is the main staple, in keeping with the environment, where nature has not yet been subjected to widespread human abuse.

The Veneto is one of Italy's most important wine-producing regions. Verona-area vineyards use only local grapes to produce such wines as Amarone, a dry red that is excellent with roasts and game; Bardolino; and Valpolicella, a red wine better suited to lighter fare. Soave is a white wine that accompanies fish; Custoza white goes well with any meal. Recioto is a sweet red wine. In the area around Treviso we find excellent *spumanti,* or sparkling wines, as well as good reds, including Cabernet, Merlot, and Raboso. These last are also produced in Portogruaro, in the province of Venice, with such other white wines as Tocai, Pinot Bianco, Pinot Grigio, and Riesling, all excellent with fish. The province of Vicenza produces Gambellara, a smooth, dry white wine. The Breganze area yields seven different wines including a Bianco, another dry white that goes well with fish; a Rosso, excellent with roasts; and Torcolato di Breganze, a sweet red.

In contrast to a world more interested in dieting than in hearty cuisine, often obsessed with the fear of overeating, the Veneto, with the exception of some industrial areas, has maintained strong ties to the earth and its products. Mealtime is highly valued as a communal time to be serenely shared with family and friends. If there is a single philosophy that governs one's life, in the Veneto that philosophy is to adhere to the simple things, as simple and down-to-earth as the Venetian people themselves.

Land of ancient forest myths and legends relegated today to the memories of its oldest inhabitants, the Trentino–Alto Adige, located at the heart of the Alps, was once a crossing point between the Latin and German worlds. In this region, two distinct populations coexist. In the north, the majority of the population is German-speaking, in the south, Italian-speaking. The two provinces have in common the lay of the land, characterized in large part by mountainous masses, the plains being limited to the low valleys of the major rivers. The provinces also share a lively tourist industry, thanks to their natural beauty and to the popularity of winter sports, as well as many products such as fruit, wine, cheese, milk, and timber. The two cuisines are quite different, however. The more Italian Trentino features both Lombardian and German influences grafted onto the cultural base of the Veneto, while Alto Adige combines German, Austrian, and Slavic influences. The cuisine of the Trentino has lost its memory of the festive banquets offered by the bishop-princes of the region to the cardinals and sovereigns who attended the Council of Trent in 1545–63, and has long been simple and austere. The soups, such as *orzetto alla trentina,* made with barley and a vast

An old woman at the market in Bolzano, the provincial capital of Alto Adige, to sell produce from her garden.

A woman harvesting Spumante and Doce grapes near Lago di Garda.

assortment of vegetables, are typical. There are *canederli,* large, ball-shaped dumplings made with bread, flour, milk, and eggs, and sometimes combined with liver, lard, or various types of salami, either cooked in a skillet with butter or served in meat broth (recipe page 26). Polenta, whether made of yellow corn or of buckwheat, is widespread. It is served with *luganeghe,* small sausages boiled or cooked on a grill, or with mushrooms, of which the province has a rich abundance. Seafood dishes are numerous. Of these, trout, tench, eel, char, barbel, and grayling head the list. The cheeses here are excellent, including *asiago, vezzena,* and various others known by the names of the localities in which they are produced. A typical Christmas dessert is *zelten,* made with flour, sugar, and raisins.

In the Trentino, vineyards are a fundamental component of the landscape, and the wines produced are of the highest quality. Among the noteworthy whites are Chardonnay, Nosiola, Pinot Bianco, Pinot Grigio, Riesling, and Traminer Aromatico, all excellent with fish; and Moscato Giallo and Vin Santo, wines for dessert or between meals. Among the reds we find Cabernet for roasts and game; the almost purple Marzemino with its characteristic velvety taste, good with roasts and white meat; Merlot to accompany stewed and grilled meat; and Pinot Nero to accompany fowl. The production of sparkling wines, born of the felicitous marriage of Pinot Nero and Chardonnay grapes, is very important in the Trentino.

One characteristic dish of Alto Adige is *knödel,* or dumplings, closely related to the *canederli* of the Trentino and stuffed with meat. There are many types of soup in this region, from snail soup to soup made with Terlano wine, from brain soup with fresh herbs to goulash of Balkan derivation. Different types of bread, almost always made with rye, accompany these soups. The thin, hard, flavorful loaves traditionally were baked before winter weather made the outdoor ovens inaccessible and in such a way that they could be kept for months. Other regional specialties include sauerkraut, polenta, mushrooms, trout, smoked meats, small sausages with pig's blood or liver, and game, the last often accompanied by preserves made from the wild berries that abound in this province. Important desserts are strudel and *zelten;* the latter, unlike the Trentino type, is made with rye flour and is much richer. This province produces greatly prized white wines, among the best in Italy.

In the Friuli region, which shares borders with Germanic and Slavic countries, two completely different cultures live together harmoniously. On the one hand, there are Trieste and Gorizia and their small inland region, with its deep Middle European roots, and on the other hand, there is the rest of the area, consisting of plains, mountains, and hills unified by a common rural culture. From this mixture derive various regional cooking styles: the inland friuliana, tied to the peasant world; the internationally influenced

◄ OPPOSITE

Simply prepared seafood dishes at the Antica Trattoria Poste Vecie in Venice: on top, cooked giant prawns (cigale di mare) and smaller prawns (gamberoni)*; in the center, dishes of squid (polpetti) and sea snails (lumache di mare)*; and some scallops (cape sante)* in the fore-ground.*

The fish market, one of many shops at the Rialto market in Venice.

Wild fruits used at the Molin Vecio restaurant in Caldogno to prepare the dish on page 19; pictured here are more *(blackberries),* fragoline di bosco *(wild strawberries), and* lamponi *(raspberries).*

triestina, combining Austrian, Slovene, Mediterranean, and even Hungarian influences, since Trieste was the great maritime center of the Hapsburg empire; the cuisine of Gorizia, also reflecting the Hapsburg presence; and, finally, the cuisine of the Adriatic coast, which shows Venetian influences. The unifying element—whether for the Triestino sea captain or for the peasant from Carnio who has emigrated abroad—is a love for the homeland, thought of as a small country, and the desire to reunite with family members around the *fogolar,* the typical hearth surrounded by benches at the center of the traditional friulan kitchen. In a region that extends from the Adriatic Sea to the Carnic Alps, with a climate that varies, assuming a Mediterranean character along the coast and a continental character on the inland plain and in the mountains, agricultural food production is varied. There are *prosciutto,* of which San Daniele and Sauris are excellent varieties; *cotechini* (sausages), among which Muset, prepared from parts of pigs' heads, is famous; and cheeses such as *montasio.* On the plain, corn is the dominant cultivar, but beans and potatoes are also important. A characteristic friulan soup is *iota,* made with beans, milk, cornmeal, and *brovada* (white turnip ripened in grape dregs). Also common are soups made from *bobici* (fresh kernels of corn), barley-

and-potato soup *alla triestina,* and bean soup *alla friuliana.* Pork, beef, and game, together with fish from the Adriatic, are the basic elements of many second courses. The entire hog is used here, from the head to the feet. The bacon is smoked, the tongue and blood are used, and the meat is ground to make various sausages and *prosciutto.* The famous goulash, a meat stew of Hungarian origin, is made from beef, as are roast beef with herbs and—from beef intestine—tripe. Characteristic desserts of this region are *strucolo,* a kind of sweet bread or strudel; and *gubana* and *pinza,* different varieties of sweet bread eaten during Easter.

The white and red wines of the Friuli region are renowned the world over. The most prized area is the Collio Goriziano, the hilly strip located between Dolegnia and Gorizia, where white wines such as Sauvignon, Pinot Bianco, Pinot Grigio, Riesling, Verduzzo, Silvaner, and a superb Tocai are all produced. Also from the Collio come prized red wines such as Merlot, Cabernet Franc, and Pinot Nero. From the Colli Orientali del Friuli which run along the Yugoslavian border come such whites as Tocai Italico, Verduzzo, and the precious Picolit, as well as reds such as Raboso and Cabernet. In addition to traditional wines, the region also produces the highly esteemed grappa, famous the world over.

Vito Quaranta

Gratin di frutti di bosco con gelato al rabarbaro, *wild fruits first heated then mixed with homemade rhubarb ice cream at the Molin Vecio restaurant in Caldogno, near Vicenza in the Veneto.*

This dish, traditional for Christmas Eve, is typical of Mantua, where pumpkin production is large. The stuffing ingredients reveal a lingering medieval taste for spice, and create an unusually sweet pasta. Because American pumpkins differ greatly from their Italian counterparts, butternut squash is substituted here.

Tortelli di Zucca   Pasta Stuffed with Pumpkin

From Gabriele Bertaiola of Antica Locanda Mincio, Borghetto di Valeggio

Serves 8

The stuffing:

Two 2-pound butternut squashes
1 egg
1 cup ground *amaretti* cookies
    or macaroons
2 cups freshly grated Parmigiano
    cheese
½ teaspoon freshly grated nutmeg
2½ cups plain dried breadcrumbs
2 tablespoons ground pine nuts
2 tablespoons raisins
¼ cup Cremona *mostarda*, pitted
    and chopped (optional)
½ cup Amaretto liqueur
Pinch of salt
1 teaspoon grated lemon peel
1 tablespoon grated orange peel

The dough:

4 cups unbleached all-purpose flour
4 eggs
Pinch of salt

The sauce:

4 tablespoons (½ stick) butter
2 tablespoons chopped fresh sage,
    or ½ tablespoon dried sage
1 cup freshly grated Parmigiano
    cheese

Preheat the oven to 400°.

To make the stuffing, cut the squashes in halves, remove the seeds and strings, and bake shell sides up on a baking pan lined with foil for about 50 minutes or until the flesh is soft when pierced with a fork. Scrape out the flesh and mash it with a wooden spoon in a large bowl until smooth. Measure out 3 cups of this flesh, drain it, then place it in another large bowl. Add the rest of the stuffing ingredients to the flesh and blend together well. For best results, store the stuffing in the refrigerator for a day before making the *tortelli*, to allow all the flavors to blend.

Make the dough with the ingredients listed, following the directions for pasta on page 247. Roll the dough a bit thicker than usual, as the filling is quite moist. Proceed with the directions on page 247 for making *ravioli*.

Cook the *tortelli* in plenty of boiling salted water for 3 or 4 minutes, until they come to the surface, then drain thoroughly. While they cook, melt the butter with the sage, making sure the butter doesn't brown.

To serve, place a layer of *tortelli* on a serving dish, pour some of the melted butter and sage on top, and sprinkle with cheese. Repeat layering until all *tortelli* and sage butter are used.   *(Photograph 1, opposite page)*

1. *Making* tortelli di zucca *(recipe left) at the Antica Locanda in Borghetto di Valeggio sul Mincio, between Mantua and Verona in the Veneto.*

2. *Gabriele Bertaiola's kitchen utensils at the Antica Locanda Mincio.*

3. *Red peppers and fennel at the Piazza delle Erbe market in Verona.*

4. *Garlic, onions, beans, and grains in the Piazza delle Erbe market in Mantua.*

5. *Sylvia going to market with the produce of her garden in Faver, just northeast of Trent.*

6. *Ovoli funghi,* mushrooms, at the market in Vicenza.

7. *Racks of a local flat bread in Bolzano, called* Schüttelbrot *in German,* pane di segala secco *in Italian.*

8. *Giant prawns* (cigale di mare), *top, and squid* (seppie), *in the Rialto fish market in Venice.*

9. *Prosciutto non cotto drying in attics in San Daniele, just north of Udine in Friuli–Venezia Giulia.*

◀ OVERLEAF
Tradition blends with the present day in the sitting room of the old Heiss Hof, a private home in the Valle Sarentina in Alto Adige.

1

2

3

4

5

6

7

8

9

Montasio is a local cheese made in the mountains near the Austrian border in Friuli. Now classified as a traditional cheese, it was being produced as early as the thirteenth century by the monks of the Moggio Abbey near Tolmezzo.

Though available in the United States in specialty cheese stores, montasio *may be hard to find. Italian* provolone *is a suitable substitute for both the* montasio *cheeses listed in the ingredients below.* Frico *can be served as a first course.*

Frico   Fried Cheese

From Gianni Cosetti of the Albergo Roma, Tolmezzo

Serves 4

1 medium onion, peeled and thinly sliced (or 1½ peeled, cored, and thinly sliced Granny Smith apples)
3 tablespoons butter
½ pound young *montasio* cheese (or Italian *provolone*), grated to yield 2 cups

¼ pound matured *montasio* cheese (or Italian *provolone*), grated to yield 1 cup
Salt and pepper to taste

Brown the onion or apple in the butter in a frying pan. Before it turns golden, add the cheese. Season with salt and pepper. As soon as the underside is crisp, turn the *frico* like an omelet and fry the other side. *(Photograph right)*

Some ingredients and the finished result of frico, *fried cheese, at the Albergo Roma in Tolmezzo in Friuli (recipe left).*

◄ OPPOSITE PAGE
Speck, *a smoked mountain ham, with a selection of local breads at the Speckstube restaurant in the Albergo Mezzavia, north of Bolzano in the Valle Sarentina. Traditionally, the kind of* albergo *where the restaurant is located catered to hunters, who would bring their own knives to eat at the inn (*speck *is used in a recipe for dumplings, page 26).*

Gianni Cosetti, a native of Tolmezzo, has been running his inn, the Albergo Roma, for twenty years. Built in 1870 as a stopping station for travelers on their way to Udine, the place maintains an Old World charm, using fine crystal and silver cutlery to serve simple, traditional foods of the area.

Polenta is a major staple of the northern Alpine regions. Its extremely simple ingredients adapt beautifully to a huge variety of accompaniments; like pasta, it is never served alone. Once boiled, it can be either fried or grilled. Polenta is recommended with seppioline nere *and* fegato alla veneziana *(recipes page 29),* toresan sofega nei funghi *(recipe page 31), and* merluzzo in cassoeula *(recipe page 83).*

Polenta   Cornmeal Gruel

From Gianni Cosetti of the Albergo Roma, Tolmezzo

Makes 2 pounds, serves 6 to 8

10 cups cold water
2 cups yellow polenta (cornmeal)
3 teaspoons salt

Boil 5 cups of water in a large pot over high heat. Mix the remaining 5 cups of cold water with the cornmeal in a large bowl, stirring rapidly. When the mixture is smooth, pour it slowly into the boiling water. Add the salt and bring back to the boil, stirring constantly. Lower to a simmer and let the polenta bubble slowly for about an hour.

When cooked, the polenta is very smooth, thick, and creamy, and pulls away easily from the sides of the pot. Pour it out on a platter, allow it to cool, then slice and use as directed.   *(Photograph right)*

A wedge of cooked polenta at the Albergo Roma (recipe left).

Mrs. Heiss in her traditional clothes in the Valle Sarentina in Alto Adige.

The most important food in Trentino–Alto Adige cooking is the pig, and the ultimate preparation of pork is speck, *which usually means smoked bacon, but in this region means boned, smoked ham. It takes three months to make first-rate* speck, *since the meat is smoked slowly and intermittently for two or three hours a day in a cold climate at high altitude. In the United States,* speck *is available at Italian specialty food stores.*

The names of dishes in this region clearly echo the influence of the Austro-Hungarian empire, which ruled here until 1918. Many names have been simply translated into Italian. Canederli *comes from the Austrian word* knödel. *These dumplings should be served in their broth topped with grated Parmigiano cheese, as a soup.*

Canederli Tirolesi Tyrolean Dumplings

From Erica Locher of Restaurant Speckstube, near Ponticino

Serves 6

3 eggs	2 tablespoons chopped parsley
1 cup milk	Salt and pepper to taste
6 cups stale white bread cubes	About 1 cup flour
(½-inch dice)	7 cups chicken or beef broth
¼ pound *speck* or *prosciutto,* finely	¾ cup freshly grated Parmigiano
chopped to yield ½ cup	cheese

Beat the eggs with the milk. Add the bread cubes, *speck* or *prosciutto,* and parsley, and season with salt and pepper. Mix well, then add enough flour to make the mixture hold together.

With wet hands, roll into balls slightly smaller than tennis balls. Bring the broth to a boil. Flour the *canederli* lightly and simmer them in the broth for 15 to 20 minutes over low heat, making sure the dumplings are covered by the broth while cooking. Serve them in their broth topped with grated cheese.   *(Photograph opposite page)*

Bottled preserves at Sergio Boschetto's Molin Vecio restaurant in Caldogno, left to right: scopeton (salacca scozzese, *Scottish fish);* tege peperoni *(tege di pevaron, pimentos and peppers);* zucchini; *and* melanzane *(eggplant).*

OPPOSITE▶
Canederli tirolesi *at the Speckstube restaurant in the Albergo Mezzavia in Valle Sarentina (recipe above).*

Some ingredients and the finished result for pasta e fagioli, *at Mr. Quaranta's home in Ronchi di Castelnuovo (recipe right).*

Pasta e fagioli *belongs to a class of dishes that unifies the nation of Italy. Practically every region has its own version. In the Veneto, it was originally made with pork fat and ham bone; today, olive oil from the Tuscan and southern versions prevails. This recipe calls for a bit of both.*

Pasta e Fagioli   Pasta and Bean Soup

From Vito Quaranta of Verona

Serves 4

1 cup dried *cannellini* beans	1 cup peeled and chopped potato
3 ounces bacon or *pancetta* chopped to yield ¾ cup	Salt to taste
⅔ cup trimmed and chopped celery	6 ounces (¾ cup) dried macaroni
¾ cup peeled and chopped carrot	Freshly ground black pepper
1 cup peeled and chopped onion	½ cup grated Parmigiano cheese
1¼ cups peeled, seeded, and chopped fresh tomatoes	Olive oil for garnish

Put the beans in a bowl, cover with fresh water, and soak overnight.

Next day, cook the bacon or *pancetta* in a frying pan, then dry it on paper towels. Drain the beans, put them into a large pot, and cover them with 6 cups of water. Add all the chopped vegetables, the bacon or *pancetta*, and season with salt. Start out over medium heat, and when the soup starts to boil, reduce heat to low. Cook, partially covered, for about 2 hours. Stir occasionally, and add some water if the soup looks too dry. When the beans are tender, add the macaroni and cook until the pasta is done, about 10 minutes.

The soup should be quite thick. Serve warm with a dusting of pepper to taste, 2 tablespoons Parmigiano cheese per serving, and a few drops of good olive oil on top.   *(Photograph left)*

Dried porcini *mushrooms are suitable in sauces and soups, but fresh ones should be used for this dish. Portobello mushrooms can be used as a substitute if fresh* porcini *are not available. Serve as a first course or side dish to stewed meat (recipe page 159).*

Funghi Porcini Trifolati

Fresh Porcini Mushrooms Stewed in Parsley and Garlic

From Gianni Cosetti of the Albergo Roma, Tolmezzo

Serves 6

1 pound fresh *porcini* or Portobello mushrooms	2 teaspoons peeled and chopped garlic
2 tablespoons olive oil	Salt and pepper to taste
1 thick slice bacon	2 tablespoons chopped parsley

Clean, rinse, and dry the mushrooms; cut into chunks.

Warm the olive oil in a pan and sauté the bacon with the garlic for a few minutes. Remove them from the pan with a slotted spoon and discard. Place the mushrooms in the seasoned oil and sprinkle with salt and pepper. Stir gently. Cover the pan and stew over low heat for about 15 minutes. Add the chopped parsley and serve.

Serve seppioline nere alla veneziana *as a first or main course, with slices of fried or grilled polenta (recipe page 25).*

Seppioline Nere alla Veneziana   Venetian Squid

From Dino Boscarato of the Ristorante Dall'Amelia, Mestre

Serves 4

2 pounds small squid, with ink
¼ cup olive oil
1 teaspoon peeled and finely
   chopped garlic
½ cup peeled and chopped onion

1 cup seeded and chopped fresh
   tomatoes
Salt and pepper to taste
1 cup dry white wine
1 tablespoon chopped parsley

If the squid is not already cleaned, remove the insides from the tube-like part of the fish, and pull out the thin transparent spine bone. Remove the purplish outside skin, which comes off very easily in warm water. Remove the small ink bags from each side of the head, but save the ink. Remove the eyes, and the hard beak-like part in the center of the tentacles. Rinse the squid thoroughly in running water (they are a milky white when clean). Cut the body of the squid into rings. If the tentacles are bigger than a mouthful, cut them in half or in quarters accordingly.

Heat the oil in a pan and sauté the chopped garlic and onion until golden. Then add the squid. After 2 or 3 minutes add the tomatoes and season with salt and pepper. When the squid is half done (about 5 minutes), pour in the wine and squid ink and continue cooking slowly. Just before they are done, sprinkle with chopped parsley.   *(Photograph above right)*

Ingredients and the finished result for seppioline nere alla veneziana at the Ristorante Dall'Amelia (recipe left).

This famous Venetian preparation for liver should be served as a main course, accompanied by slices of fried or grilled polenta (recipe page 25).

Fegato alla Veneziana   Venetian Liver

From Dino Boscarato of the Ristorante Dall'Amelia, Mestre

Serves 4

2 large onions, peeled and cut into
   thin rings
2 tablespoons olive oil
4 tablespoons (½ stick) butter
Salt and pepper to taste

1½ pounds calf's liver, sliced very
   thin
1¼ cups dry white wine
¼ cup chopped parsley

Soak the sliced onions in ice water for 10 minutes and drain them well.

Heat the oil and butter together over medium heat in a large frying pan. Sauté the onion until translucent, then season with salt and pepper. Add the liver to the pan and sauté quickly, a few minutes per side. Sprinkle with wine and cook for another 2 minutes. The liver should be moist and just barely pink when cut. Add the parsley, stir, and serve.   *(Photograph right)*

Fegato alla veneziana (recipe left) at the Ristorante Dall'Amelia in Mestre, the mainland gateway to Venice.

Toresan, *pigeon in the local dialect, is a specialty around Vicenza. Traditionally the birds used in this recipe were so young that they had not yet learned to fly, and so tender that they would melt in the mouth along with the subtle flavor of the* porcini *mushrooms.*

This dish is seasonal, and reaches its peak in August and September. There is a local saying, de agosto, colombo rosto, *or "in August, roast pigeon."*

Toresan Sofega nei Funghi Squab with Mushrooms

From Sergio Boschetto of Molin Vecio, Caldogno

Serves 4

4 young squab, feathered, washed, and dried (reserve livers, hearts, and gizzards)
2 medium slices bacon, cut in halves
4 fresh sage leaves, or ½ teaspoon dried sage
4 sprigs rosemary, or 1 teaspoon dried rosemary
1 cinnamon stick, broken in 4 pieces
4 cloves
4 small shallots, peeled
Coarse salt
Freshly ground pepper
6 tablespoons olive oil
2 tablespoons butter
4 juniper berries
½ cup trimmed and chopped celery
½ cup peeled and chopped carrot

¼ cup chopped *pancetta* or bacon
1 cup dry white wine
Beef broth
⅔ cup peeled and thinly sliced onion
Pinch of flour
Dash of red wine
1 pound fresh *porcini* or Portobello mushrooms, washed, dried, and chopped
1 teaspoon peeled and finely chopped garlic
3 tablespoons chopped parsley
Pinch of ground thyme

1 pound precooked polenta (½ of recipe on page 25)

Stuff each bird with ½ slice of bacon, 1 sage leaf (or ⅛ teaspoon dried sage), 1 sprig rosemary (or ¼ teaspoon dried rosemary), 1 piece of cinnamon, 1 clove, 1 shallot, and 1 pinch each coarse salt and freshly ground pepper. Tie the birds securely.

In a large, deep skillet, sauté the birds in 1 tablespoon olive oil and 1 tablespoon of the butter, together with the juniper berries. Add the chopped celery, carrot, and *pancetta;* after a few minutes add the white wine. Cover the skillet and cook on low heat for about 40 minutes, turning the birds often and adding broth from time to time to maintain a sauce.

In the meantime, boil the squab gizzards in lightly salted water until they are cooked through, about 5 minutes; drain and cut into chunks. In a frying pan, sauté the gizzards for a few minutes with the hearts, livers, and the thinly sliced onion, in 1 tablespoon of butter. Sprinkle the flour and red wine into the pan, season with salt and pepper, and cook for a few minutes longer. Remove from the heat, blend the mixture until smooth, pour into a saucepan, and set aside. This sauce will be used as an additional dressing.

Sauté the mushrooms with the chopped garlic and parsley in 4 tablespoons olive oil for about 10 minutes. Season with salt and thyme.

Preheat the oven to 475°. Slice the polenta and cook the slices in a frying pan in 1 tablespoon olive oil over medium heat until crispy and golden on each side, about 10 minutes altogether. Dry on paper towels.

When the birds are done, cut them in half and arrange them in a large baking dish. Strain the cooking juices and pour over the birds. Cover with the mushrooms, and bake in the oven for 2 or 3 minutes. Warm the gizzard sauce. Serve the birds hot with the gizzard sauce and polenta.

◄ OPPOSITE PAGE
Ingredients for toresan sofega nei funghi *at Sergio Boschetto's Molin Vecio restaurant in Caldogno (recipe left).*

Preserves of peaches at the Antica Locanda in Borghetto di Valeggio sul Mincio.

Torta di Mele   Apple Cake

From Gabriele Bertaiola of Antica Locanda Mincio, Borghetto di Valeggio

Serves 6 to 8

The filling:

4 cups peeled, cored, and thinly
    sliced Granny Smith apples
2 tablespoons fresh lemon juice
¾ cup Calvados or applejack
½ cup sugar
1 tablespoon flour
½ teaspoon freshly grated nutmeg
1 teaspoon grated lemon peel
1 tablespoon grated orange peel
6 tablespoons fresh orange juice
2 tablespoons butter, cut in small
    pieces, plus extra to prepare
    the pan

The pastry:

2¾ cups flour
1 cup sugar
½ pound (2 sticks) butter, cut in
    small pieces
4 egg yolks
Pinch of salt
½ teaspoon grated lemon peel
1 tablespoon ice water

Confectioners' sugar

Place the apple slices in the lemon juice in a large, shallow bowl and cover with the Calvados. Let macerate for 1 hour. Drain before using.

To make the pastry, put the flour on your work surface or in a mixing bowl and make a well in the center. Add the sugar, butter, and egg yolks. Sprinkle salt and grated lemon peel for the pastry around the edges of the well. Knead together quickly, adding ice water if necessary to make a workable dough. Let to rest for 30 minutes in the refrigerator. Roll out the pastry in 2 round disks, 1 slightly larger and 1 slightly smaller than your pan.

Preheat the oven to 400°.

Put the larger round of pastry in a buttered 9-inch deep dish or springform pan. In a bowl, mix together the sugar, flour, and nutmeg for the filling and spread them on the pastry. Sprinkle with lemon and orange peel, then cover with the apple slices and sprinkle with orange juice and pieces of butter. Cover with the other pastry round and press down around the edges to seal. Pierce the top with a fork in a few places, then bake for 40 minutes.

Sprinkle confectioners' sugar on top of the cake, and serve warm.

(Photograph opposite page)

A gondoliere in traditional dress on the Grand Canal in Venice.

OPPOSITE►
Some ingredients and the finished result for torta di mele *at the Antica Locanda in Borghetto di Valeggio sul Mincio (recipe above).*

The market on the Piazza Mazzini in Chiavari in Liguria.

Farinata, *a flat bread made with oil and chickpea flour, as sold in the street at Giuseppe Bonino's Osteria Luchin in Chiavari.*

◄ OVERLEAF
A view of the Isola di San Giulio across Lago d'Orta, from the town of Orta in Piedmont.

II. *Liguria / Piedmont / Valle d'Aosta*

Iₙ a restaurant in one of Liguria's many rose and pistachio-painted towns, there is a cook whose pasta is so fine that through it the wild herbs in its stuffing are almost as clear as on a botanist's chart.

"We Ligurians are the Scots of Italy," she said one day. "Like them, we lost our kingdom to our neighbors—to Savoy, in 1815. Like them, we are thrifty—too cheap even to buy our own salt, we dip our bread in the sea instead. In Genoa, though, they are so tight it would take two Scots to make one Genoese!"

Liguria is no longer the great nation of seafarers that produced Columbus. More money is made now on the Italian Riviera from commercial flower cultivation and from tourists. But Liguria's people still dip their bread in the sea. Their most emblematic dish, *cappon magro*, began as a ship's biscuit soaked in sea water, and doused with olive oil—the lean (*magro*) meal Genoese sailors ate while their masters feasted on *cappon* (castrated cockerel). It has evolved over the years into a Vesuvian display of all the best in this new moon of mountainous coast cradling the tough old port of Genoa.

The base of *cappon magro* remains a biscuit soaked in salt water. Then come tender vegetables, what fresh fish there is (never plentiful on this coast, and usually bony), sometimes *musciame* (strips of dried dolphin once prepared by sailors aboard ship, still for sale by Genoa's docks) or *bottarga* (pressed, sun-dried roe of tuna or gray mullet), and finally a crown of mollusks and crustaceans, the whole edifice moistened with a green sauce of pounded herbs, anchovies, and olive oil.

Many of Liguria's dishes were conceived over the centuries by lonely Ligurian women as celebrations of their men's return from long voyages at sea. Nineteenth-century food shops deep in Chiavari's medieval honeycomb of arcades display such architectural delights as *torta pasqualina*, an Easter pie in which artichokes are cooked and mixed with ricotta and Parmigiano cheese, then poured into a vast, multilayered pastry shell.

Arrive in Chiavari early on market day and you may find *farinata* (called *socca* in Nice), a breakfast crepe of chickpea flour mixed with olive oil and baked in a wood-burning oven, or a great dimpled slab of *focaccia*, the bread most typical of Liguria (a paper-thin version is the specialty of the town of Recco, recipe page 58): flat, once-risen dough flavored with coarse salt, shredded onion, cheese, or pulped olives.

All the markets on this warm Mediterranean coast are full of oranges, lemons, apricots, bilberries; tiny vegetables to be stuffed and fried as in Nice—for Liguria is essentially a vertical garden trapped between sea and mountains, a geographical isolation that has forced it, historically, to turn away from Italy toward its maritime trading partners.

Driving the two-hundred-mile road that links the Riviera di Ponente (abutting the French Riviera in the west) to the Riviera di Levante (running east from Genoa to Tuscany, with its glimpses of Renaissance villas and seaside resorts), or walking the rugged coastal path around five almost inaccessible southern Ligurian towns known as the Cinque Terre, one sees and smells the region's primary culinary ingredients before tasting them. In early spring, when borage's first violet flowers bloom, the young leaves add their cucumber taste to *ravioli* stuffing. Later, market stalls will have a wild herb blend called *preboggion*, found only in Liguria. It is usually made of lovage, sorrel, wild chicory, borage, and chervil, but may also include dandelion, pimpernel, and young thistle shoots. Lightly cooked and mixed with *prescinsena* curd cheese, it fills the region's best pasta—*pansoti*, triangles or squares of an egg and white wine dough served with a coarsely ground walnut sauce, *salsa di noci* (recipe page 57).

Marjoram is the queen of herbs here, but basil rules. Basil *pesto* (recipe page 57), pounded with garlic, salt, pine nuts, olive oil, and *pecorino*, ewe's milk cheese, as dear to the Genoese as their wallets, is the condiment that the Ligurians call their "flag." It originated in Persia, perhaps transplanted to this coast by Phoenicians. Ligurians had long traded with the East, and the Greeks and Phoenicians established trading posts at Genoa as early as 500 B.C., yet no Persian liaison could have the fragrance that Liguria's fruity oils impart; the olive trees which step up its precipitous terraces are said to imbibe the salt and sweetness of the sea breezes. Nor could another *pesto* be as aromatic. Genoa's spicy short-leaved basil is picked when no more than three inches high, before the flowers bud, to prevent its color darkening on contact with hot food. The grassy, chlorophyll-green *pesto* that results is used as a sauce for *gnocchi*, and to stir into vegetable soups, or to dress a corkscrew pasta called *trofie* that is cooked and tossed with French beans and potatoes.

Perhaps it was *pesto*'s color that first attracted Ligurian sailors, for the Eastern spices that lured them away in trade seem to have filled them with an intense nostalgia for the green flavors of home. One of the few Middle Eastern skills they adopted was that of crystallizing fruit, an art refined to such a degree that in the last century most of Europe's royal houses kept a purveyor of candied fruit in Genoa. The sugared gems still appear in everything from domed cakes known as *pandolce* (precursor of the showier and better-known *panettone di Milano*) to a strange but delicious Renaissance recipe in which *ravioli* are stuffed with candied pumpkin, bone marrow, and orange peel.

I found the relic of another Renaissance tradition in a small Chiavari shop crowded with carved ships' figureheads and classical plaster busts. Next to them lay what looked like a pile of wooden coins. "I make them for our ancient pasta, *corzetti*," said a man I took for the shopkeeper, "each stamped with a coat of arms." He looked sadly around. "All these carvings are mine. When I was younger, I dreamed of being a Michelangelo, a Donatello! Instead I am famous as the last man to carve *corzetti*.

"Still, it is good to be famous for something!" he grinned, and sat down to carve my initials onto a mold (recipe for *corzetti*, page 54). He would accept nothing in return—proof, if it was needed, that the Ligurian's reputation for parsimony owes less to truth than to a certain self-mockery.

Tajarin, *a local kind of* tagliatelle, *made at Mr. Rocca's Ristorante Giardino da Felicin in Monforte d'Alba in Piedmont.*

OPPOSITE ▶
Tagliatelle, *perhaps the most common cut of pasta in Italy, as it is made by Mr. Lorusso at his Ristorante La Cròta in Roddi in Piedmont (directions for how to make a basic egg pasta are on page 247). The use of many eggs is characteristic of the pasta making of this region.*

Rane con funghi e cornetti, *frogs' legs with mushrooms and beans, served at Piero Bertinotti's Ristorante Pinocchio in the town of Borgomanero in Piedmont.*

In late autumn in Piedmont, the foothills of the Alps, one smell dominates—and it is not basil. It hangs heavily in Alba's main street; it lurks in Turin's turn-of-the-century restaurants; it so outrages some Italian society that it is banned on public transport; yet it is largely responsible for Piedmont's current position as gastronomic center of Italy.

When ready to spread its spores, that most princely of the potato's cousins, *tuber magnatum,* the white truffle of Alba, begins to give off a musky aroma powerful enough to penetrate its nest in the soil around the roots of trees. To put it bluntly, the thing reeks of sweat; more precisely, of androstenone, the essential oil found in male sweat. Hence its attraction for female pigs.

Pigs being difficult to train, their place in the truffle world has been usurped by dogs, who hunt not for love's sake but for hunger's. "If they are not hungry," said Omberto, who holds the equivalent of a Ph.D. in truffling, "truffles could be as big as chairs and the dog would be off after the first bitch in heat."

For the whole month of October, Alba, center of Piedmont's wine and truffles, and hence its culinary capital, holds its annual truffle fair, the most important of many gastronomic festivals. The wiliest truffle hunters bring their prizes to town every weekend to auction off to buyers from all over the world, and every serious restaurant in Piedmont puts truffles on the menu. I was invited once for an *assaggio* (a tasting) of truffles, which I imagined innocently would be a light lunch.

The gastronomically unfit should beware of invitations to "tastings" in Piedmont. First there is a long wait, while the unwary nibble at hand-rolled breadsticks known as *grissini*, a specialty of Turin. They are about a yard long, thin, and irregular, some rolled in fine semolina, some flavored with crushed hazelnuts.

A dish appears, a simple one of marinated *ovoli reale* mushrooms ("royal eggs"—because of their shape and regal flavor). With it, a yellow pepper stuffed with basil, tuna, capers, hard-boiled egg, and anchovies. This slips down easily. Next, a plate of finely chopped raw veal ("*sanato*—the best in Italy, killed while still milk-fed," one is told), tartened with lemon juice at the last minute, to prevent discoloration, then dressed with olive oil, garlic, and black pepper, and lacquered with shaved truffles.

Carne cruda all'albese. Raw meat, Alba fashion.

More and more plates arrive. A bowl of melting fontina cheese, *fonduta*, with layers of truffles buried in its depths. A platter of deep, purpley-red *risotto al Barolo* flecked with truffles ("The secret is to put the wine in first—one whole bottle of Barolo!" says the chef. Recipe for white wine *risotto*, page 51). A giant

Carne cruda, *or* carpaccio al gorgonzola, *made by Piero Bertinotti at the Ristorante Pinocchio in Borgomanero. This is actually a simple preparation of thinly sliced raw beef dressed with a sauce of mild gorgonzola cheese, cream, eggs, lemon, vegetable oil, vinegar, and salt.*

raviolo in which a nest of truffles cradles an egg yolk. Some *porcini* mushrooms the size of salad plates, grilled over a chestnut fire so they taste like steak coated in savory custard, anointed with truffled oil. A *bagna cauda* (warm bath) of olive oil, garlic, and anchovies, at the center of a sunburst of raw vegetables (recipe page 54). Then a casserole of wild hare stewed in Barolo "à la civette," highly perfumed with juniper, nutmeg, cloves, surrounding a lesser Alp of polenta—coated, once again, in a blizzard of truffles.

The host smiles encouragingly, "Only three more dishes."

If this is one of the feasts for which the region is famous, there may be *bui* to follow, a grand *bollito misto* traditional for New Year's. It must contain five different boiled meats at the very least, with a quartet of vivid sauces: a red tomato "bath," the *bagnet tomatiche;* a honey and ground walnut sauce called *saussa d'avie;* a *salsa verde/bagnet verd* of garlic, parsley, anchovies, and bread; and *mostarda d'uva,* a spicy mix of candied fruit and mustard syrup (recipe for *bollito misto* with *salsa verde,* page 130).

When pigs were killed just once a year, at the onset of winter, there would always be a feast given to consume those parts that could not be preserved. Thus the *gran fritto misto* evolved, in which the offal is dipped in egg and crumbs, then fried in butter and olive oil with sweetish semolina fritters, wild mushrooms, apple, and chocolate-flavored milk cream.

The orgy of eating may seem excessive, but such overindulgence is a result of past privation. "Even as late as the 1940s," I was told, "there were peasants in the mountains suffering from rickets because for months they had only polenta to eat" (polenta, a New World gift to the Italian poor from Columbus, recipe page 25) "—rubbed, if they were lucky, with an anchovy."

Those possessing a goat or a flock of sheep would not have starved, of course. The high hills of Alta Langhe developed many dishes based on its ewe's milk *toma* cheese (called "di Murazzano" when made within a small circle of villages). It is often served as a first course, usually when it is no more than a week old and still redolent of the herbs the sheep have eaten, its flavor sharpened by a sauce of parsley, olive oil, and chiles. Before olive oil became widely available, the oils used would have been walnut and hazelnut.

At the end of a meal a gritty and close-grained *toma* appears, the result of two to three months' aging under oil. Or there may be fragrant *formaggio con latte,* a rare, month-old cheese proved for another month under cow and sheep milk, then eaten with a spoonful of its own creamy liquid.

Recipes from that poor kitchen, *la cucina povera,* make up *Nonna Genia* (*Grandma Genia*), a cookbook published by a club known as the Cavaliers of the Truffles and Wines of Alba. They meet once a month in country trattorias to eat rustic regional dishes, legacy of more austere times, and to keep alive their rich traditions and dialect, usually in the form of songs performed by a Piedmontese poet and winemaker. "Though his poems are better than his wine," as one friend said. Their language is like something heard in the streets of Old Nice, a reminder that Garibaldi, hero of Italy's struggle for Unification, was born in that city, before it was ceded to France by the puppet-master, Camillo Benso, Conte di Cavour, in the *Risorgimento* of 1849–61.

1. *All kinds of nuts in the market at Porta Palazzo in Turin, the capital of Piedmont.*

2. *A man harvesting Dolcetto grapes in Albaretto, northwest of Cuneo in Piedmont.*

3. *A variety of olives at the market in Turin.*

4. Cima ripiene alla genovese, *stuffed veal with ham and eggs, served with campagna bread in Chiavari.*

5. *The famous breadsticks of Turin, called* grissini.

6. *Trays of chocolates at Peyrano, one of several famous chocolate shops in Turin, the birthplace of the European chocolate industry in the eighteenth century.*

7. Agnolotti al pizzicotto, *butterfly-shaped meat-and-vegetable–stuffed pasta at the Ristorante La Cròta in Roddi.*

8. *A variety of local cheeses with a bottle of Barolo wine at the Ristorante Giardino da Felicin in Monforte d'Alba.*

9. *Limes, red and yellow raspberries, strawberries, blackberries, blueberries, small kiwis, gooseberries, and a large prickly horned melon at the Ristorante da O'Vittorio in Recco in Liguria.*

1

2

3

4

5

6

7

8

9

The mantle of poverty was shrugged off too recently not to have left chafe marks. Superficially, Piedmont resembles Tuscany with a backdrop of Alps: the same vineyards striping the country like corduroy, the same medieval hill towns. On closer inspection the Piedmontese towns are less sybaritic, the tourists intent on buying Barolo rather than villas. People here are more reserved—peasants who bought their farms and vineyards with profits from the recent wine boom, or with a son's factory wages.

Tuscany is Italy's Bordeaux; it has that region's large wine estates and aristocratic families. Piedmont, birthplace of the modern Italian state, is Burgundy, with its countless stubbornly independent producers and minor nobility—and unlike Tuscany, whose many cities are dedicated to art, Piedmont has a single metropolis: Turin, the hardest-working place in Italy, dedicated to Fiat.

For a city where the car is king, Turin is surprisingly elegant, its vast arcaded piazzas reminiscent of de Chirico's surreal cities. Equally surprisingly, the one-time capital of French Savoy (from 1559 into the nineteenth century) has few dishes of its own, perhaps because its cooks, unlike those in the countryside, were for so long influenced by the French court.

With the exception of *grissini*, Turin's specialties are for the sweet-toothed. *Zabaione* was invented here in the seventeenth century, when a royal chef accidentally spilled fortified wine into some custard. So were *marrons glacés* (despite the French name)—Europe's best chestnuts, *marroni*, as distinct from the less succulent *castagne* (known as poor man's bread), come from Val di Susa, outside Turin. The fame of the city's chocolatiers was such that the Swiss came to study their art, but they did not stay long enough to master the Turinese blending of butter, chocolate, and the *tonda gentile della Langhe* (a round, gentle hazelnut of the Langhe which accents so many sweets here) into a rich cream known as *gianduia*. When formed into individual chocolates, these are *gianduiotti*, best sampled in one of the city's glittering cafés with a quick *bicerin*, a blend of coffee, cream, and sweetened hot chocolate served in something like a Russian tea glass.

At Turin, the wooded hills and mountains of Cuneo and the Langhe join the vast Lombard plain, the breadbasket of Italy, producing rye, barley, maize for polenta, wheat, and oats, as well as sixty percent of the country's rice, which explains the abundance of *risotto* recipes in Piedmont.

Directly north of Turin is the beautiful Valle d'Aosta, where the Mont Blanc and St. Bernard passes meet. To this the region owes its historic importance. Its capital, Aosta, was founded by Roman lords to keep at bay their hot-headed Gaulish neighbors. Aosta's straight Roman streets today are ruled by higher, more permanent lords—Mont Blanc, Mount Rosa, the Matterhorn (*Cervino* in Italian), and the Gran Paradiso. To these high Alpine pastures the cattle of Piedmont are trucked every summer. The cows' milk, rich from

A window box in Ameno, near Lago d'Orta in Piedmont.

OPPOSITE▶
A valley scene near Gressoney-Saint-Jean, a resort in the Lys Valley near the Swiss border in Aosta.

a diet of mountain grass, produces the finest fontina cheese—next to skiing, Aosta's best-known product.

Valdostana cooking is not for the cholesterol-conscious. At a festival held annually in honor of the town of Arnad's tasty pork fat preserved in spices and Alpine herbs, an old man grinned at my slightly dismayed interest, then shaved a layer of palest pink *lardo* onto a doorstop of warm *pane nero,* the local rye and wheat flour bread (it enriches most of the region's soups, including the famous cabbage and cheese *soupe valpellinentze*).

"Mange m'tite!" he ordered, in something closer to Provençal French than to Italian.

I ate, and licked my greasy fingers, and delightedly ate some more while the old man laughed. The same herbal flavor underlined a fried *boudin* sausage, Italian cousin of all black puddings. And the same dark rye bread, thinly sliced this time, reappeared as a bed for a creamy sweet custard called *fiandolein,* flavored with a hefty slug of rum and plenty of grated lemon zest.

*An old shepherd with his dog and goats near Verrès,
a fourteenth-century fortress town in the Valle d'Aosta.*

*On Sacro Monte, this hand painted on
the wall gives directions to the next
chapel. Twenty chapels were built during
the seventeenth and eighteenth centuries
on this hill offering lovely views of the
town of Orta and its lake, below.*

This is not elegant cooking, but it is good in its way. The people here get their climbing strength and their livelihood from animal protein. They have always raised cattle for cheese and butter rather than meat, and at one time the animals were not killed until they were on their last legs, and correspondingly tough as hikers' boots. The meat was then simmered for hours to produce the strong broth essential to Valdostana soups, and finally preserved in wooden barrels with garlic, herbs, and salt, to be enjoyed throughout the long winter. This preserved beef is the ripe, earthy flavor in their classic *carbonade* stew. In such wild mountains, game and freshwater fish are understandably important. Rarer now is *camoscio,* a wild chamois goat stewed and served with polenta, or cured to make a smoky *prosciutto* known as *mocetta.*

The Valdostana people are proud of the cultural ambivalence resulting from their position at the junction of Italy with France and Switzerland. But somewhere in these remote valleys that ambivalence resolves itself, and the land of Dante and Michelangelo gives way finally to William Tell and the Napoleonic code.

The truffle which scents Piedmont scents its complex, assertive red wines as well. Perhaps this is more than coincidence, for neither the red Nebbiolo grape nor the white truffle flourishes outside Piedmont—and before the days of concrete vineyard supporters, truffles were often found next to the vine.

Piedmont has more DOC zones (*denominazione di origine controllata,* equivalent to France's *appellation contrôlée*) than any other region in Italy and yet produces less volume, concentrating its creativity on two of the world's aristocrats—the austere and muscular Barolo and its rounder, more velvety counterpart, Barbaresco—and two day-to-day "people's wines"—Barbera and Dolcetto. The once-renowned Gattinara from north of the Po River is only just recapturing a reputation it lost over the last decade. Both Barolo and Barbaresco get their aging ability from the Nebbiolo grape, but producers differ as to whether this aging should be done in a cask, as tradition dictates, or in a bottle, for a lighter wine that peaks earlier. Dolcetto and Barbera are the wines found most often on Piedmontese tables. "Analyze Piedmontese blood," I was told, "and you will find more than half of it is Dolcetto." Good producers of Barbera are often those famous for their Barolos and Barbarescos, which the best Barbera resembles.

Red grapes usually occupy the best and sunniest upper slopes of the Langhe and Monferrato hills, but Piedmont makes more money from Vermouth—and produces more white wines, in particular the sparkling Asti Spumante (although locals prefer Moscato d'Asti). A fairly recent rediscovery of old vines near Alba has resulted in the deliciously almondy Arneis.

White wine dominates Liguria as well, but its best wine, Rossese di Dolceacqua, found near the border with Provence, is a bright ruby red, reminiscent of wild berries and crushed flowers. Very little is exported, even by the largest producers, although it is less rare (but more deserving of its reputation) than the legendary white Cinqueterre. Only the slightly sweet Sciacchetra from the Cinqueterre area is worth tracking down. Grown on terraces built by Roman slaves, it has a flavor said to be a result of the Mediterranean breakers that wash its vines.

Other collector's wines are those of the Valle d'Aosta, the highest vineyards in Europe, where the names are French but the style Italian. Two of the most exalted owe their preservation to the clergy: Blanc de Morgex, a delicate greeny-gold wine with herbal notes, resurrected after years in decline by a village priest; and the white dessert wine Malvoisie de Nus. But Valle d'Aosta wine will never be more than a curiosity. More typical, perhaps, is the *grolla* passed around after dinner, a carved, many-spouted bowl filled with coffee and laced with fiery grappa.

Leslie Forbes

OPPOSITE▸

Sculptures by Donigo Bussola depicting the canonization of Saint Francis, in one of the chapels on Sacro Monte near the town of Orta.

The quality of Piedmont rice was already famous in 1787, when Thomas Jefferson is said to have smuggled some out of the country and to have brought the first Piedmontese rice to America. In Italy risotto *is served as a first course.*

Antico Risotto Sabaudo   White Wine Risotto

From Danilo Lorusso of the Ristorante La Cròta, Roddi

Serves 6

2 tablespoons butter	1 cup white wine
1 cup peeled and chopped onion	6 cups heated chicken or beef stock
½ cup cooked ham cubes (¼-inch dice)	¼ pound fontina cheese, chopped in ¼-inch dice to yield ¾ cup
1 teaspoon chopped fresh rosemary, or ¼ teaspoon dried rosemary	¼ cup grated Parmigiano cheese
2 cups Arborio rice	Meat gravy (optional)
	White truffle (optional)

A serving of antico risotto sabaudo *with shavings of white truffle at the Ristorante La Cròta in Roddi (recipe left).*

Melt the butter in a large pot and sauté the onion until soft. Add the ham cubes and cook until just warmed, about 1 minute. Then add the rosemary and rice and stir until the butter is absorbed. Add the wine and simmer until it evaporates; then add enough stock to cover the rice, and stir.

Keep adding hot stock as it is absorbed into the rice, continuously stirring well with a wooden spoon. When the rice is about half-cooked (after 10 minutes), add the fontina cheese and cook about another 10 minutes, continuing to add stock as needed. Finally, add the Parmigiano cheese, a few spoonsful of gravy if desired, and serve. Grate white truffle generously over all, if available.   *(Photographs above right and opposite page)*

◄ OPPOSITE PAGE
Some ingredients and the finished result for the classic Piedmontese dish antico risotto sabaudo *at the Ristorante La Cròta (recipe above left).*

Borragine, or borage, has always been said to have exhilarating properties, and to give courage. It has a pronounced flavor of cucumber.

Friscoë   Fritters

From Gianni and Vittorio Bisso of the Ristorante da O'Vittorio, Recco

Serves 6

1 package dry yeast	2 cups trimmed and chopped borage, or peeled and grated cucumber
½ cup warm milk	
4 cups all-purpose flour	Salt to taste
⅓ cup peeled and finely chopped onion	Vegetable oil for frying, enough to come ½ inch up the side of your frying pan
1 egg	

Add the yeast to the warm milk and leave for 15 minutes to activate.

Mix the yeast/milk with the flour, onion, egg, borage or cucumber, salt, and 2 cups water. Use a wooden spoon or a blender at a low speed to make a very soft, almost runny dough. Leave to rest for about 1 hour in a large bowl covered with a damp dishcloth.

Heat the oil in a frying pan. Since the dough is quite runny and sticky, first dip a spoon into the hot oil and then take tablespoonfuls of dough and drop them into the oil. Turn the fritters in the pan and as soon as they are lightly browned on both sides, remove them from the oil and drain on paper towels. Serve immediately.   *(Photograph page 52)*

A man smelling a truffle, valued at approximately $85, to check its quality at the truffle fair held every October in Alba.

Friscoë, *fritters (recipe page 51), and ver-*
dure ripiene alla genovese (recipe right)
at the Ristorante da O'Vittorio in Recco.

Verdure ripiene, *stuffed vegetables, is a traditional dish of Liguria. In the days*
before home ovens, housewives prepared their vegetables and took them to the
local baker. When he had finished baking bread but still had a nice hot oven,
in went the verdure ripiene. *Just before midday one would see women return-*
ing home carrying large dishes wrapped in colorful mandilli, *dishcloths knot-*
ted at the ends to make a handle. Today these vegetables are served as a first
course.

The eggplant used in this recipe is the small Italian variety; if it is unavail-
able, substitute an additional quartered sweet pepper.

Verdure Ripiene alla Genovese

Stuffed Vegetables, Genoese-style

From Gianni and Vittorio Bisso of the Ristorante da O'Vittorio, Recco

Serves 4

2 pounds small white onions, peeled and cut in half	Milk to soak the bread
1 pound small Italian eggplants, trimmed and cut in half lengthwise	½ cup freshly grated Parmigiano cheese
1 pound small zucchini, trimmed and cut in half lengthwise	½ cup ricotta cheese
1 sweet pepper, quartered, seeded, and deveined	2 eggs
1 small white bread roll, cut in half	Pinch of marjoram
	Oregano
	Salt to taste
	Olive oil

Wash the vegetables and boil them individually in salted water until *al dente,*
then drain and cool.

Remove 1 or 2 inner layers of the onions. Core the eggplants and zucchini, leaving at least ¼ inch of shell, and discard the eggplant pulp. Put the
zucchini pulp and inner onion layers in a bowl. Dip the bread in some milk,
squeeze dry, and put in the bowl.

To make the stuffing, chop the zucchini pulp and inner onion layers
together with the bread, then add the Parmigiano and ricotta cheeses and
mix with a wooden spoon. Finally, add the eggs, a pinch of marjoram and
oregano, and salt to taste, and mix thoroughly (do not use a blender).

Preheat the oven to 475°.

Fill the vegetable shells (the zucchini, onion, eggplant, and sweet pepper
pieces) to the top with stuffing and place them in an oiled baking dish, leaving about ½ inch between the shells. Dribble a few drops of olive oil on each
and garnish with a pinch of oregano. Bake for 20 to 25 minutes, or until
golden on top. Put the *verdure* on a serving platter and pour the juices from
the dish on top. Serve warm, or at room temperature in the summer.
(Photograph above left)

A selection of frittura mista *(fried*
seafood) at the Ristorante da O'Vittorio:
totani *(squid),* acquadelle *(anchovies),*
mazzancolle, *and* scampetti *(two kinds*
of shrimp).

OPPOSITE ▶
The interior of Mulassano, a popular café/bar in Turin.

Uncooked *paste at the Ristorante da O'Vittorio, from top to bottom:* trofie, pansoti, *and* corzetti, *a coin-shaped pasta (recipe right).*

Corzetti *is a typical pasta of Liguria. The wooden utensil used in the restaurant to make this coin-shaped pasta was roughly two inches in diameter and carried a carving of the Bisso family coat of arms, which created grooves in the pasta to hold the sauce.*

Corzetti   Coin-shaped Pasta

From Gianni and Vittorio Bisso of the Ristorante da O'Vittorio in Recco

Serves 6

The pasta:	The topping:
2 cups unbleached all-purpose flour	2 tablespoons butter, melted
1 egg	*Salsa di noci* (recipe page 57)
¼ to ⅓ cup water	½ cup grated Parmigiano cheese
Pinch of salt	

Make the pasta dough with the ingredients listed above, following the directions on page 247. Let sit for about 10 minutes. Roll out with a rolling pin to the thickness of a penny (the dough will be soft). Cut into disks, using a round utensil about 2 inches in diameter, with grooves carved into it to imprint the dough. (If such a utensil is unavailable, cut the dough using a glass or round cookie cutter with a 2-inch diameter, and then imprint the rounds of dough by pressing down on them with the back of a fork.)

Cook the *corzetti* in plenty of boiling salted water. When they rise to the surface, drain thoroughly. Put them on a large platter, and toss the *corzetti* with the melted butter, *salsa di noci,* and grated cheese to serve. *(Photograph above left)*

OPPOSITE PAGE►
Ingredients for bagna cauda *at the Ristorante La Cròta in Roddi (recipe below right).*

When serving bagna cauda, *one should have plenty of coarse red wine on hand to wash it down, and lots of crusty Italian bread to mop up the drippings.*

Bagna Cauda   Hot Dip

From Danilo Lorusso of the Ristorante La Cròta, Roddi

Serves 6 to 10

24 anchovy fillets packed in oil	5 or 6 cloves garlic, peeled
1 cup olive oil	A variety of raw vegetables
3 tablespoons butter	

Wash and chop the anchovy fillets.

Heat the oil and butter in a large pot (preferably an earthenware pot). Slice the garlic very fine, add it to the pot, and heat over low heat, stirring constantly with a wooden spoon until the garlic is just soft—it must not brown or become too golden. Add the anchovies and continue stirring over low heat until they just dissolve, about 10 minutes.

Serve the *bagna cauda* hot with any fresh raw vegetables, appropriately prepared in dipping-sized morsels. Peppers, celery, carrots, cauliflower, mushrooms, broccoli, spring onions, even boiled potatoes are recommended. In Piedmont, cardoons called *cardi* are especially favored.

The dip should be kept warm at the table, but should not continue to cook after it is prepared.   *(Photographs left and opposite page)*

Bagna cauda *with a selection of fresh local vegetables and fresh bread to be dipped, at the Ristorante La Cròta (recipe right).*

The original recipe for pesto *used* pecorino *cheese, simply because Liguria used to exchange its coal for Sardinia's pecorino. Today some people prefer the lighter taste of Parmigiano, so chefs can compromise and use half and half. If Sardinia's pecorino is not available, pecorino romano can be substituted, though it is a bit stronger in flavor. If you have the time and energy to use a mortar for this and the following recipe, it is well worth the effort.*

Serve pesto *over most any pasta, with* gnocchi, *or stirred into* minestrone. Pesto *can be stored in the refrigerator, but make sure there is oil on top or the beautiful green will darken.*

Pesto   Basil and Pine Nut Sauce

From Gianni and Vittorio Bisso of the Ristorante da O'Vittorio, Recco

Serves 6

1 teaspoon coarse salt, or to taste	¼ cup chopped pine nuts
3 large bunches fresh basil, washed, dried, stems removed, and chopped to yield 2½ cups	2 tablespoons freshly grated Parmigiano cheese
3 teaspoons peeled and finely chopped garlic	2 tablespoons freshly grated *pecorino* cheese
	10 tablespoons olive oil

Pound the coarse salt in a large mortar, then add the basil and garlic. Add the pine nuts and continue pounding until the mixture is thoroughly blended. Pound in the cheeses and, finally, the olive oil, and mix well. (This sauce can also be made in a blender or food processor, though you should mix in the cheese and oil by hand after blending the other ingredients, for a better texture.)   *(Photographs below right and opposite page)*

Like pesto, salsa di noci *can be served over almost any pasta. In Liguria* salsa di noci *is served with the local* ravioli, *or with* corzetti *(recipe page 54).*

Salsa di Noci   Walnut Sauce

From Gianni and Vittorio Bisso of the Ristorante da O'Vittorio, Recco

Serves 6

2 teaspoons peeled and finely chopped garlic	½ cup heavy cream
1 teaspoon salt	10 tablespoons olive oil
1 cup chopped walnuts	2 tablespoons freshly grated Parmigiano cheese
2 tablespoons chopped pine nuts	

Pound the garlic with the salt in a large mortar. Add the walnuts and pine nuts and pound until smooth. Stir in the cream, and then little by little beat in the olive oil. Finally, stir in the Parmigiano. (This sauce can also be made in a blender or food processor.)   *(Photograph right)*

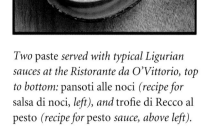

Two paste *served with typical Ligurian sauces at the Ristorante da O'Vittorio, top to bottom:* pansoti alle noci *(recipe for* salsa di noci, *left), and* trofie di Recco al pesto *(recipe for* pesto *sauce, above left).*

 ◀ OPPOSITE
Ingredients and the finished result for Gianni Bisso's pesto sauce at the Ristorante da O'Vittorio (recipe above, top).

Focaccia con Formaggio   Oven-baked Bread with Cheese

From Gianni and Vittorio Bisso of the Ristorante da O'Vittorio, Recco

Serves 6

1 package dry yeast
2 cups warm water
Pinch of sugar
5 to 6 cups white flour
¼ cup olive oil, plus extra to prepare
   the pan and dress the *focaccia*

1 tablespoon salt
2 pounds *stracchino* or Bel Paese
   cheese, broken into ¾-inch pieces
   to yield 6½ cups

Add the yeast to the water with sugar and leave for 10 minutes to activate.

Mound 5 cups flour on a large work area or in a large bowl. Make a deep hole in the top of the mound, pour in the yeast/water, ¼ cup of oil, and salt. Add a little more flour if the dough is unmanageable, though it should be quite thin. Knead until smooth. (This can also be done in a food processor.) Let the dough rise for 1 hour in a large bowl covered by a damp dishcloth.

Cut the dough in half and roll out 2 rounds. The rounds should be as thin as possible and able to fit on your baking pan, on top of each other.

Preheat the oven to 500°.

Put 1 round of dough on the well-oiled baking pan, and press down to eliminate air pockets. Arrange the cheese pieces on top, in concentric circles, starting from the outer edge. The pieces of cheese should be ¾ to 1 inch apart. Place the other round of dough on top, press the edges to seal, and cut the excess dough with a pasta or pastry wheel. Pinch the top of the dough with your fingers 4 or 5 times, tearing it slightly, to prevent the *focaccia* from "inflating." Finally, dribble a few drops of olive oil on top. Bake the *focaccia* for no more than 7 or 8 minutes. Serve hot.   *(Photograph above left)*

Cooked and uncooked focaccia con formaggio *at the Ristorante da O'Vittorio (recipe right).*

OPPOSITE PAGE▶
Some ingredients and the partial preparation for torta salata *at the Ristorante La Cròta (recipe for a similar* torta, *below right).*

Torta Autunnale di Verdure   Fall Vegetable Pie

From Danilo Lorusso of the Ristorante La Cròta, Roddi

Serves 6

1½ pounds zucchini
Salt
Olive oil to prepare the pan
1 pound puff pastry
2 whole eggs and 3 egg yolks
3 tablespoons freshly grated
   Parmigiano cheese

½ cup ricotta cheese
Pepper to taste
Pinch of nutmeg
1 cup cooked ham cubes
   (½-inch dice)

Preheat the oven to 350°.

Wash the zucchini, trim the ends, cut into ⅛-inch-thick disks, salt lightly, and place in a colander to drain. Oil a 9-inch pie pan. Roll out the puff pastry into a circle slightly larger than the pan, and place it in the pan.

Beat the eggs and yolks together in a medium-sized bowl, then fold in the cheeses. Add salt and pepper to taste, the nutmeg, and the ham. Spread the mixture evenly around the bottom of the unbaked puff pastry. Cover with the zucchini disks.

Bake the pie for 40 minutes, or until the filling is puffed and toasted on top. Serve warm.   *(Photographs left and opposite page)*

A completed torta salata *made with mushrooms, zucchini, Parmigiano cheese, and Swiss chard at the Ristorante La Cròta (recipe for a similar* torta, *right).*

Cooked brasato al Barolo *at the Giardino da Felicin (recipe right).*

The following dish is excellent served as a main course with mashed potatoes or braised carrots on the side.

Brasato al Barolo   Beef Braised in Barolo Wine

From Mr. Rocca of the Ristorante Giardino da Felicin, Monforte d'Alba

Serves 6

2 cloves garlic, peeled
1 teaspoon chopped fresh rosemary,
    or ¼ teaspoon dried rosemary
3 tablespoons olive oil
1 cup peeled and chopped onion
1 cup trimmed and chopped celery

1½ cups trimmed, peeled, and
    chopped carrot
2 pounds chuck roast, securely tied
Salt and pepper to taste
2½ cups Barolo wine

Very finely chop the garlic and rosemary together. Pour the olive oil into a pot large enough to hold all of the ingredients. Sauté the onion until translucent, then add the celery and carrot. Sauté the vegetables until soft, then add the garlic and rosemary and sauté a moment longer.

Put the meat in the pot, brown on all sides, and add salt and pepper. Pour in the wine and simmer, covered, over low heat for 2 hours, or until tender.

Remove the meat from the pot. Pour the liquid and vegetables into a blender or food processor and blend to make a thick sauce. Reheat the sauce, then slice the meat and serve with the sauce on top.   *(Photograph left)*

Fagiano Caldo in Carpione   Pheasant with Shallot Sauce

From Piero Bertinotti of the Ristorante Pinocchio, Borgomanero

Serves 4

One 3-pound oven-ready pheasant
2 teaspoons chopped fresh rosemary,
    or ½ teaspoon dried rosemary
2 teaspoons chopped fresh thyme,
    or ½ teaspoon dried thyme
1 teaspoon chopped fresh sage,
    or ¼ teaspoon dried sage
½ cup trimmed and chopped celery
1 cup peeled and chopped onion

½ cup peeled and chopped carrot
2 tablespoons olive oil
2¾ cups dry white wine
2 tablespoons butter
¼ cup peeled and finely chopped
    shallots
2 tablespoons vinegar
2 egg yolks, beaten
Salt and pepper to taste

Some ingredients and the partial preparation for fagiano caldo in carpione *at the Ristorante Pinocchio (recipe right).*

Stuff the pheasant with the herbs. Sauté the celery, onion, and carrot in the oil in a large flameproof casserole, then add the pheasant and brown on all sides. Add the wine, a little water if necessary to cover the bird, and bring to a boil. Cover the casserole and simmer over low heat for 1 hour.

While the pheasant is cooking, melt the butter in a small pan and sauté the shallots until soft and golden. Set aside.

Remove the pheasant from the casserole when done. To make the sauce, strain the juices from the casserole, then boil them with the vinegar and shallots in a saucepan until reduced to about ⅓ of the original volume. Stir a couple of tablespoons of the hot liquid into the 2 egg yolks, then, off heat, stir the yolks into the reduced liquid. Whisking constantly, heat gently until the sauce is slightly thickened. Season with salt and pepper. Joint the pheasant and serve with the sauce poured on top. (For a smoother sauce, liquefy in a blender and strain before adding egg yolks.)   *(Photograph left)*

Triglie alla Ligure   Red Mullet with Olives

From Gianni and Vittorio Bisso of the Ristorante da O'Vittorio, Recco

Serves 2

Two 8-ounce red mullets, cleaned
  and scaled (or small red snapper)
¼ cup olive oil
½ cup white wine
Pinch of salt

¼ cup small black olives, or thinly
  sliced large black pitted olives
2 teaspoons peeled and finely
  chopped garlic
2 tablespoons chopped parsley

Preheat the oven to 350°.
Place the fish in a baking dish. Pour the olive oil and wine over the fish, then
add the salt and olives. Cover with foil and bake for 15 to 20 minutes, or until
the fish flakes easily.
    Sprinkle with garlic and chopped parsley and serve.
(Photograph right)

Triglie alla ligure, *raw and cooked, at the
Ristorante da O'Vittorio (recipe left).*

*A view of the hill town of Chiama and the mountain behind
at sunset, looking from Levanto, in Liguria.*

*The Bolsieri family sitting down to All Saints' Day lunch at their farm,
Ca' de Pinci, near Canneto sull'Oglio, just east of Cremona.*

*Cooking by the fireplace in the dining
room of Franco Colombani's Albergo del
Sole, in Maleo.*

◄ OVERLEAF
*Ducks and geese kept by the Santini family in a stream behind
their Ristorante Dal Pescatore in Canneto sull'Oglio.*

III. *Lombardy*

Lombardy is an intricate mosaic of cities and countryside, nine very different provinces that form the largest and richest region in Italy. From snowy Alpine mountains and austere foothills to the rich farmland of the Po Valley, where green fields of wheat, soy, rye, and corn are planted as neatly and intensely as are the poplars whose thin trunks form an elegant screen across the countryside, Lombardy refuses to be easily categorized. It sweeps from the rice-growing Lomellina region at the edge of Piedmont past the unforgettably beautiful lakes Maggiore, Como, and Garda to the ducal city of Mantua, set in a silent landscape at the eastern border near both Emilia-Romagna and the Veneto. Each of these provinces, dotted with castles, farmhouses, cathedrals, and citadels, has been shaped by its special geography, which virtually guarantees the immense diversity of Lombardy's cooking. A description in the 1931 classic *Gastronomic Guide to Italy* makes the region sound (in a very broad translation) like one of the inner zones of paradise: "From its fertile soil come abundant grains and vegetables of all varieties, fruits and vines cover its hillsides . . . its mountains are thick with game, its rivers and lakes with fish . . . its plains and Alps a rich pasturage for the raising of cows on a vast scale, whose milk produces the famous cheeses and butters for which Lombardy is known."

The Po may be the most important river not only of Lombardy but also of northern Italy, although many other watercourses link the region. Icy Alpine streams flow into the lowlands; subterranean springs become lakes in which pike, carp, perch, and tench thrive. From the many rivers lacing the region come freshwater fish such as eel and sturgeon, while waters in canals irrigate meadows and inundate the rice fields which became home to the frogs, shrimp, and tiny fish that give up their flavors to *risotti* and sauces for polenta. These canals were once busy routes of commerce through which the major traffic of the region moved. The Naviglio Grande, constructed after Barbarossa's destruction of Milan in 1154, is an ancient link between the city and the countryside, and its clear waters still flow into a charming, if gentrified, artistic neighborhood of Milan that is full of attractive restaurants. Now the various watercourses that linked the region are mostly forgotten; it seems a mere curiosity that they were once so important that young women's dowries often included ownership of canals as well as a box at La Scala.

I have been particularly lucky to see Lombardy through the eyes of a friend whose love of his region informs everything he does. Antonio grew up in the center of Milan, fascinated by the smells of *cassoeula* or of tripe cooked in the streets by workers maintaining the tram tracks. As a child he began exploring the city, wandering past old arches, ancient churches, and old houses with hidden secret gardens into kitchens where the fragrance and tastes of *risotto* golden with saffron, steaming bowls of *minestrone,* and platters heaped high with soft meatballs called *mondeghili,* with fish *in carpione,* and *ossobuco alla milanese* captured his attention and have had it ever since.

Extending his explorations, he bicycled into the countryside, stopping to catch local fish in the streams and cook them over a simply built fire. As a child he fell in love with the tiny town of Maleo, where, many years later, he was married at the Albergo del Sole. Franco Colombani, the owner of this singular inn and country restaurant, has a library of ancient books and documents from which he researches regional dishes. With great respect for tradition, he keeps the culinary culture of Lombardy alive while carefully reinterpreting it with a modern sensibility. He makes balsamic vinegar in his own *acetaia* and gets cheese and produce from the finest sources in the surrounding countryside (including such proud locals as the old man I saw arriving one morning with a still-thrashing eighteen-pound pike in his canvas satchel).

Dairy cows on the Ca' de Pinci farm of the Bolsieri family, near Canneto sull'Oglio.

Mascarpone, *a rich triple cream cheese, being made at the Consorzio Latterie Sociali Mantovane, a cooperative in Mantua where farmers bring their milk to be made into cheese and sold directly to distributors.*

Lombardy gets its name from the Lombards, a tribe of barbaric Germanic warriors who picked up what pieces were left of the disintegrated Roman empire and set about fortifying the countryside with encampments. Food was hardly a major legacy. Their only culinary contribution was *pollo alla creta*, chicken slathered in clay, cooked in the embers of the fire, and then served by cracking open the hardened shell to remove the feathers and reveal a succulent bird within. *Faraona alla valcuviana*, guinea fowl cooked the same way, is still made in the Brianza district just north of Milan.

It was enterprising French Cistercian monks who started the great cheesemaking tradition of Lombardy in the twelfth century when they began to reclaim the marshlands and irrigate the vast sweep of flatland in the fertile plain of Lombardy. Once drained, the land became pasture for dairy cows and for the cattle whose meat goes into the roasts, stews, and *bolliti misti* of the region. By the fifteenth century much of the countryside had been planted with wheat, rye, and spiky green shoots of rice by the Visconti and

Provolone *and* rigatino *cheeses hanging and aging at the Isola Dovarese cheese cooperative in Cremona.*

Sforza, Gonzaga and Este families, the dynastic rulers of the region. It was they who laid the foundations for later nobles and wealthy merchants who created country estates in the eighteenth century to retreat from the steamy heat of summer and to farm the fertile countryside. These men revolutionized farming and the landscape when they created the *cascine,* the monumental stone and brick farms sprinkled across the flat alluvial plain. The tile-roofed *cascine* enclose an entire agricultural world that shelters the dairy cows and cattle so important to the cuisine of the region as well as the cattle whose meat becomes its rich stews and *stracotti.*

From just such a farm came *zuppa pavese,* which was invented for the French King Francis I after his defeat in 1525. On the way from Pavia to prison, his captors stopped at the farm of a poor man and asked for a meal, explaining that they had a king in their entourage. To honor such a guest, the wife brought out all the culinary riches she had. She sautéed bread in butter like a *crostino,* warmed some broth to boiling, slid in a raw egg that poached in its heat, dusted the soup with grated *grana padana* cheese, and set the meal before the king.

He was neither the first nor last ruler to eat well in Lombardy. Wars and revolutions, the French, Spanish, Hapsburgs, Napoleon, and the Austrians followed one another, leaving their culinary signatures in the dishes by which we know Lombardy today. Weave these convolutions of power into a landscape of luxurious vegetation, and there are gastronomic consequences: rich, complex dishes for nobles, such as those served at the court in Mantua, one of the most splendid in sixteenth-century Europe, and, at the other extreme, dishes of extreme simplicity that relied on tastes of whatever wild herbs, greens, or grains the countryside yielded up.

The cuisine of Mantua, in particular, still has traces of the opulent banquets of the Gonzaga family in the sixteenth century, when forty-five courses constituted a dainty dinner. Some dishes with the Venetian and Oriental flavors of the Renaissance appear at table only at Christmas, but the restaurant Il Cigno thoughtfully preserves tastes of the city's culinary patrimony all year long in serving *agnolini, ravioli* filled with boiled beef or capon, marrow, cinnamon, cloves, cheese, and eggs; *tortelli di zucca,* pumpkin-filled pasta that is sweet and aromatic with *mostarda* and *amaretti* cookies (recipe page 22); and *insalata di cappone,* capon salad with its tantalizing sweet and sour flavors (recipe page 77). Il Cigno's chefs and other chefs and cooks like them are aided in their devotion to preserving the noble traditions of the past by drawing upon the great resource of the books of Bartolomeo Sacchi, known as Platina, and Bartolomeo Stefani, who was chef at the Gonzaga court and author of *L'Arte di ben cucinare* in 1662.

Lombardy's wealth did not save peasants and farmworkers from living at the edge of poverty. Their diets relied on polenta and other grains of the poor and on soups like the *minestrone* of Milan, a dense mixture of beans, vegetables, herbs, *pancetta,* and tiny *pastine;* or the numerous simpler *minestre di riso,* rice soups, which combine rice with bitter greens, or pumpkin, cabbage, wild greens, beans, fish, or chicken livers.

Polenta has always been the food of the poor, especially in the north of Lombardy (recipe for polenta, page 25). It is as versatile as *risotto* or pasta, and like them, its various flavorings and accompaniments vary from valley to valley. It was originally made of whatever minor grains were available—millet, buckwheat, or spelt—and became a popular dish only after yellow corn was introduced to Europe by Columbus. Cornmeal polenta reached Lombardy a century later in the wake of its enthusiastic reception in the Veneto, and was soon cultivated, since corn grew well where no other plant would take root. The steamy fragrance of polenta still wafts through country households, where it is made in the great bucket-shaped copper pot called a *paiolo.* It is then poured in a creamy mound onto a wooden board, or cooled, sliced, and grilled, or reheated with a sauce. Alessandro Manzoni, in *I promessi sposi,* described polenta as "looking like a harvest moon in a large circle of mist." The glowing golden polenta moon is delicious by itself, but it becomes the vehicle par excellence for sauces which it absorbs, or is an accompaniment for all the meat and fish dishes of the region. Steaming mounds of *polenta e osei,* polenta and little birds, are comfort food for people in Brescia and in Bergamo, who are so enamored of the combination that they dreamed up the trompe l'oeil *polenta e osei* dessert, a simple cake shaped like a bowl of polenta, covered with almond paste, and crowned with little chocolate game birds encircling its crest.

Until early in this century, every farm family had its own pig, and pork in its many guises is still a favored meat of the region. It turns up as sausages and *salame,* especially in the area just north of Milan, which produces *salame di Milano,* as *luganega de Monza,* and in the *salamella* from Cremona. Lombardy has a taste for the lesser meats, poor people's food transformed into dishes with sublime taste: tripe, which

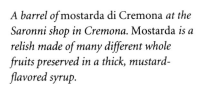

A barrel of mostarda di Cremona *at the Saronni shop in Cremona.* Mostarda *is a relish made of many different whole fruits preserved in a thick, mustard-flavored syrup.*

An exhibit of work from the Scuola Internationale di Liuteria, in the window of a violin shop in Cremona.

An array of classic Lombardian sausages: salamini dei morti, cotechini, salsicce, *and* zampone. *These sausages might be simply cooked with cabbage, onion, and celery, as shown here at the Albergo del Sole in Maleo.*

A suckling pig ready to be cooked at Peck's Bottega del Maiale in Milan.

finds its apotheosis in the delicate soup called *busecca; cassoeula,* a stew with cabbage to which the ears, feet, and rind of the pig contribute their taste; and *fritto misto alla milanese,* a mixed fry which includes brains, liver, and lungs.

Anyone who has ever feasted on its cheeses or tasted its butters, its rich meats, and its polentas knows that the kitchen of Lombardy can be a kitchen of cholesterol. Butter is the cooking fat used almost universally and meat, especially veal and beef, is a frequent presence at table. We can taste the influence of France in Milan's use of cream—rich Milanese took their cooks to Paris in the nineteenth century—and see the hand of Austria in the way that meat is slowly stewed or braised. And we can certainly detect Austrian organization in the meticulously planted fields of the region.

Cheeses are made in every part of Lombardy from the high Alpine pastures where cows and goats graze to the *cascine* of the fertile plain of the Po. They are part of a highly organized industry, which contributes to Lombardy's remarkable prosperity, as well as an artiginal tradition whose farmhouse cheeses are great resources of the region. Fine gratings from wheels of granular Parmigiano-like *grana padana,* which has been made in the region for a full ten centuries, are dusted over *minestre*, pastas, and *risotti*. Blue-veined Gorgonzola, from the town of the same name, comes as an ivory-colored creamy sweet cheese or in a more pungent aged version. Bland Bel Paese and Lombard *provolone* are familiar exports. Creamy *stracchino*, soft *taleggio*, *quartirolo*, or runnier *robiola* are all members of the same family, made from the milk of cows left to graze in pastures with wild plants and herbs. *Mascarpone*, the delicate fresh triple cream, may originally have been a kind of ricotta, according to a document from Como in 1168. It is now used mostly for sweets. Many of the cheeses of the Valtellina and Val Gerola mountains—*bitto, bagoss, casera*, and goat's milk *sciumudin*—are known only in Lombardy.

The Lombards are especially attached to *risotti*. They have cultivated rice since the fifteenth century and they consistently eat more of it than pasta or polenta. The short-grained rice grows through the flatlands around Milan (whence the famous *risotto alla milanese*) and near the famous pinnacled and polychrome Charterhouse at Pavia, where monks created *risotto alla certosina* by flavoring rice with the crayfish, shrimp, freshwater fish, and frogs pulled from its streams and from the water covering the fields during the long months of the growing season. Farther to the east, Mantua's singular *risotto alla pilota* was created by rice huskers, who were known as *piloti*. More pilaf than *risotto,* the grains of rice are poured into

Various salumi, *cured meats of Lombardy:* pancetta, culatello, salame, coppa, *and* cacciatorino. *Wine and some fresh bread, like the* rosetta, panino all'olio, *and* miccone *pictured here, make a fitting accompaniment to the meats as served by Mr. Colombani at the Albergo del Sole.*

Some farmhouses and a small vineyard near Domodossola.

the cooking pot to form a cone, which is almost totally covered with water and allowed to cook without being disturbed in any way. It is served with a local garlic- and spice-scented sausage called *pesto*. A simple list of *risotti* with the tastes of the countryside would have to include a version from Monza with sausage, *risotto con le rane* with frogs from Lomellina, another from Lake Como using perch, and *risotto alla vogherese*, made with sweet red peppers.

Clearly there is no single style of cooking in Lombardy since the region has as many styles as it has provinces. Three—Pavia, Cremona, and Mantua—are in the plain; Sondrio is in the mountainous Valtellina; and two others are in the lake areas of Como and Varese. The aristocratic town of Bergamo, and nearby Brescia, were both under the sway of Venice for hundreds of years and their food still reflects that influence, while Milan, the capital, has many specialties of its own.

Milan is unquestionably the gastronomic capital of Italy, although the cosmopolitan city seems to have lost all interest in its own traditions. Its hundreds of restaurants and trattorias serve food from every region and are constantly creating new culinary sensations to entice sophisticated eaters. The *nuova cucina* of Gualtiero Marchesi, whose elegant restaurant shaped the Italian eating experience of the 1980s, has been somewhat eclipsed, while the *paninoteca*, a sort of shrine to the sandwich, has taken on the shape of a major trend in this fast-paced city where work habits are much more American than Italian. Milan is home to Peck, an empire of food shops in the center of the city, an institution as great in its own way as the Duomo or Galleria. It includes a delicatessen with virtually all the finest cheeses, sausages, and salami of the country; a shop devoted only to products of the pig, and another solely to cheeses; and a take-out emporium with spits full of every known variety of poultry cooking in front of a wood-burning fire. The restaurant Peck serves impeccably cooked food based on the ingredients sold at its shops.

Typical Milanese dishes include *risotto alla milanese* made with beef marrow and saffron (recipe page 79); *ossobuco*, braised veal shank served with *gremolada*, a sprinkling of grated lemon and chopped parsley and garlic (recipe page 80); *busecca*, a tripe dish of surpassing subtlety; and *costoletta alla milanese*, a breaded and fried veal chop which the Milanese claim inspired the Austrians to create Wiener schnitzel. Many Milanese specialties were created in the Renaissance when doctors believed that gold was good for the heart. Meat and poultry dishes arrived at table shimmering in finely beaten gold, so capturing the hearts of the Milanese that by the seventeenth century they were even covering bread with gold. Poorer people clearly needed a substitute ingredient so they tried dipping dishes in beaten eggs—hence *costoletta*, a meatball in a golden crust—and added the golden tint of saffron to *risotto* and in the process created *risotto alla milanese.*

Three cities lie in the heart of the Po Valley. Pavia is set beyond the Po on the south side of the river, where the frogs that swim in its waters and in the rice fields are soon transformed into *rane in guazzetto,* frogs' legs stewed in a tomato sauce flavored with herbs and wine. Ludovico Sforza encouraged the raising of geese in nearby Lomellina, so that the animals could live in happy proximity to the rice fields and so that he and all the ruling dukes of Milan could feast on goose. Jewish communities made the first goose salami, *salame d'oca,* during the Middle Ages, although today's version is about one-third goose, one-third lean pork, and one-third pork fat or *pancetta* and gets its haunting flavor from a variety of spices that include black pepper and coriander.

Cremona, famous for its violin masters and its elegant brick and terracotta *palazzi,* serves *marubini,* curly edged *ravioli* filled with braised meats, beef marrow, and Parmigiano cheese, and is known for both its *torrone,* a nougat of honey and almonds that has become the national Christmas sweet, and for *mostarda,* candied fruits in a sweet and spicy piquant mustard sauce, meant to be served with boiled meats.

With high mountains protecting the lake region from cold northern weather, olives, lemons, and wine grapes thrive in the vine-covered hills that stretch from Brescia to Lake Garda. At Garda the countryside is dotted with silvery gray olives which produce a much-sought-after light oil and with groves of citrus trees of which D. H. Lawrence once wrote that the oranges were like "the lights of a village along the lake at night, while the pale lemons above are the stars."

The lakes of Lombardy, with their green shoreline, lush gardens, and beautiful fishing villages, are among our most memorable images of Italy. Trout, salmon trout, and carp, celebrated by Catullus and brought to the imperial tables of Rome, are pulled out of the waters of Garda while Lake Como serves perch, a type of shad called *agoni,* and especially *misoltitt,* shad dried in the sun, layered in special barrels, and then gently revived with a bath of red wine, grilled, and sprinkled with vinegar or with *salsa verde.*

The hearty specialties of the mountainous Valtellina are as rustic as its Alpine climate and rugged landscape would suggest. *Bresaola,* air-dried beef much like *prosciutto,* and *violini,* salted and cured hams

The Piazza delle Erbe market in Mantua.

from kid, are always served as *antipasti. Pizzoccheri,* buckwheat lasagne noodles cooked with potatoes, cabbage, and garlic, are served with tangy *bitto* cheese while buckwheat polenta, *polenta taragna,* is tossed with butter and cheese.

Man may not live on bread alone, but Italians cannot live without it. The famous bread of Como is still celebrated throughout the region as much for its ineffable taste, which is usually attributed to the water, as for its delicate crunchiness. The Milanese are lost without their *michette,* the hollow crusty rolls that are perfect containers for the salami and cheeses of Lombardy.

Panettone was probably born as the Christmas bread of Milan in medieval times, when bakers enriched the dough of daily bread, which they called *panett,* by adding butter, eggs, sugar, and sultana raisins, to make a big, dense festive loaf which they naturally named *panettone.* In the 1920s, a Milanese baker named Angelo Motta wrought a revolution when he used natural yeast in the dough, which he poured into high-sided cylindrical baking forms, producing the tall-domed delicate breads we know today as the national Christmas bread of Italy. (The *colomba* of Pavia is almost identical to the *panettone,* although this Easter version is shaped like a dove and covered with a crunchy coating of crystallized sugar and toasted whole almonds.)

Although Lombardy is not among Italy's major wine-producing areas, several DOC zones produce fine wines. Fifteen different wines from the sloping vineyards of the Oltrepo Pavese, the zone south of the river Po, include hearty reds with exotic names such as Barbacarlo and Buttafuoco, and whites such as Pinot Grigio and Riesling.

The wines of the Valtellina, between Lake Como and Lake Garda, are divided into two categories: the wines of the upper slopes, made entirely of the Nebbiolo grape, and wines from the valley, which are blended with thirty percent of other grapes. The Valtellina Superiore wines are aged at least two years, and their evocative names, which come from the zones of production, are Grumello, Inferno, Sassella, and Valgella. Sfursat, a garnet-colored, highly alcoholic Amarone-like wine, is a robust wine made by allowing the Nebbiolo grapes to shrivel in full sunlight on the vine.

Memorable wines from Franciacorta, in the provinces of Brescia and Lake Garda, include Pinot Bianco, an elegant fruity dry white, Franciacorta Rosso, a graceful red, and a number of complex and elegant table wines made by Ca' del Bosco and Bellavista. Sophisticated eaters in the region may choose to drink the wine of other regions with the food of Lombardy, but they and most Italians celebrate with the Spumante of Franciacorta, both white and rosé, which are among the most appealing and finest Champagne-style sparkling wines made in Italy.

Carol Field

A bottle of Vino Santo from 1877 at the Albergo del Sole, the perfect dessert accompaniment for the various sweets shown on the opposite page.

OPPOSITE ▶

Cakes, biscuits, and candies at the Albergo del Sole in Maleo, counterclockwise from the top: croccante, biscotti, torrone, tortionata, margherite di stresa con e senza cacao, *and* pasta frolla.

Insalata di Cappone   Capon Salad

From Franco Colombani of the Albergo del Sole, Maleo

Serves 4

1 pound cooked boneless capon,
  chicken, or turkey meat, cut into
  strips
2 tablespoons raisins, soaked in
  water
1 tablespoon finely chopped candied
  citron or lemon peel
2 tablespoons fresh lemon juice

½ teaspoon salt
¼ teaspoon pepper
6 tablespoons extra virgin olive oil
1 tablespoon balsamic vinegar
1 tablespoon wine vinegar
Salad greens, seasoned to taste with
  salt and pepper

Put the poultry strips in a bowl and add the drained raisins, chopped candied peel, lemon juice, salt, and pepper. Stir in the oil and vinegars, and let sit for 1 to 2 hours.

Serve on individual plates on a bed of seasoned salad leaves.
(Photograph opposite page)

Maccheroni alle Verdure   Macaroni with Vegetable Sauce

From Franco Colombani of the Albergo del Sole, Maleo

Serves 4

¼ cup plus 1 tablespoon olive oil
1 cup peeled and chopped onion
4 cups unpeeled and chopped
  eggplant (1-inch dice)
¾ cup chopped canned plum
  tomatoes, drained
1 teaspoon peeled and finely
  chopped garlic
¼ pound green beans, trimmed

Salt to taste
1 cup diced green pepper
1 tablespoon chopped fresh oregano,
  or 1 teaspoon dried oregano
Pepper to taste
¾ pound macaroni
¼ cup freshly grated Parmigiano
  cheese

The ingredients and finished result for maccheroni alle verdure *at the Albergo del Sole in Maleo (recipe left).*

Put ¼ cup olive oil in a large frying pan over medium heat and add the onion, eggplant, tomatoes, and garlic. Let simmer over low heat until the eggplant and onion are tender.

Meanwhile, cook the green beans in simmering salted water until they are crisp-tender; drain and set aside. Sauté the green pepper in a small frying pan with 1 tablespoon of olive oil until soft, and sprinkle with the oregano. Add the green pepper to the simmering eggplant and onion when they are almost done, season with salt and pepper, and cook for another 5 minutes.

While the sauce is simmering, cook the macaroni in plenty of boiling salted water until *al dente,* stirring occasionally. Drain the pasta and put it in a serving bowl, cover with the vegetable sauce and green beans, and turn gently. Top with the Parmigiano cheese.   *(Photograph right)*

◀ OPPOSITE
The ingredients and finished presentation for insalata di cappone *(recipe above, top) at the Albergo del Sole. Mr. Colombani's version of this capon salad is derived from a recipe in the seventeenth-century cookbook pictured here.*

Tagliatelle con uovo e tartufo *at the Albergo del Sole (recipe right).*

There is great debate among gourmets about how truffles should be served. Some say with tagliatelle, *others say on eggs. This version brings the two together to make a delicious compromise.*

Tagliatelle con Uovo e Tartufo

Tagliatelle with Egg and Truffle

From Franco Colombani of the Albergo del Sole, Maleo

Serves 4

1 pound fresh *tagliatelle*
4 egg yolks
¼ pound (1 stick) butter, melted
White truffle

Cook the *tagliatelle* in plenty of boiling salted water for a minute or 2 (for directions to make fresh *tagliatelle* see page 247). Cook the whole egg yolks in butter in a small pan until just firm. Drain the pasta when done, and divide equally among 4 warm individual shallow soup bowls. Pour the melted butter over the *tagliatelle,* then place an egg yolk on top of each serving. Finally, grate the truffle generously over the top of each, and serve. *(Photograph left)*

Franco Colombani in the courtyard of the Albergo del Sole with his dog Al and a basket of chiodini *mushrooms.*

Filetto di Maiale all'Aceto Balsamico e Rafano

Pork Fillet in Balsamic Vinegar and Horseradish Sauce

From Chef Fulvio De Santa of the restaurant Peck, Milan

Serves 4

Eight 2½-ounce pork fillets or thin chops
2 tablespoons butter
2 teaspoons peeled and coarsely chopped garlic
¾ cup white wine
½ teaspoon salt
¼ teaspoon pepper

¾ cup chicken or vegetable broth, or water
1 teaspoon tomato paste
1 teaspoon balsamic vinegar
1½ tablespoons prepared horseradish, or fresh horseradish, grated and soaked in ice water

Sauté the pork fillets in the butter with the garlic in a medium-sized skillet. As soon as the pork is nicely browned on both sides, remove the garlic. Pour in the wine and cook gently until it reduces to about 2 tablespoons. Season with salt and pepper, and remove the fillets from the pan.

Add the broth to the juices in the pan, along with the tomato paste. Cook until the sauce thickens. Finally, add the balsamic vinegar.

Arrange the fillets on a serving dish or on individual plates. Pour the sauce on top and sprinkle with horseradish. Serve at once.

The use of zafferano *(saffron)* as a spice has ancient origins. Presumably the Arabs were the first producers of saffron, since the name comes from a Persian-Arabic word, zahfaran, or crocus. The Romans used it to perfume theaters, and it was deemed good for the health, especially as a remedy for, or protection against, the plague.

Each autumn-flowering crocus contains only three edible pistils, so genuine saffron is very expensive. The price of saffron varies widely according to its quality and country of origin; be on the lookout for a good deal.

In Northern Italy, butter was and still is much more widely used than olive oil for cooking. For risotto, *butter is a must.* Risotto alla milanese *is traditionally served with* ossobuco *(recipe page 80).*

Risotto alla Milanese Saffron Rice

From Pier Giuseppe Penati of the Ristorante Pierino, Viganò

Serves 6

8 cups chicken or beef broth, or water	¼ teaspoon powdered saffron, dissolved in 2 tablespoons warm broth
6 tablespoons butter	
⅓ cup peeled and chopped onion	2 teaspoons salt
1 tablespoon beef marrow (optional)	Pepper to taste
2 cups long-grain or Arborio rice	¾ cup grated Parmigiano cheese
½ cup dry white wine	

A basket of chiodini *mushrooms fresh from the garden at the Albergo del Sole. Mr. Colombani will use olive oil and the cloves, peppercorns, cinnamon, nutmeg, and bayleaf shown here to preserve the* chiodini.

While heating the broth in one pot, melt 4 tablespoons of butter in another large pot over medium heat; then sauté the chopped onion in the butter until pale gold. Adding the beef marrow at this stage gives the *risotto* a richer quality, but is not necessary.

Add the rice to the onion and stir with a wooden spoon until the rice is well coated with the butter. Add the wine and stir until it is almost all absorbed. Next, pour in enough heated broth to cover the rice, and stir. Keep the rice on medium heat, stirring and scraping the bottom of the pot constantly. As the broth is absorbed, add more of it to the rice, about ½ cup at a time, and continue to stir.

When the rice is done, it should be creamy and the grains should be tender yet firm—this will take about 20 minutes. Stir in the saffron/broth until the rice is evenly colored and flavored. Season with salt and pepper.

Stir ½ cup of the cheese and the remaining 2 tablespoons of butter into the rice. Serve topped with the remaining cheese, with *ossobuco.* (Photographs pages 80 and 81)

Franco Colombani's preserved chiodini *mushrooms at the Albergo del Sole in Maleo. These will be served as an antipasto.*

Ossobuco means "bone with a hole." It is a small veal shank, complete with its marrow, dressed with herbs and lemon. This is a very famous dish, which the Milanese pair with risotto alla milanese *(recipe page 79)—one rare occasion in Italian cuisine when the first and second courses are served together.*

Ossobuco Veal Shanks

From Pier Giuseppe Penati of the Ristorante Pierino, Viganò

Serves 4

3 tablespoons flour
4 slices veal shank, each 2 inches thick
4 tablespoons (½ stick) unsalted butter
2 tablespoons vegetable oil
⅓ cup peeled and finely chopped onion
½ cup dry white wine

Veal stock or water
½ teaspoon salt
¼ teaspoon pepper

The *gremolada:*

¼ cup finely chopped parsley
1 tablespoon grated lemon peel
1 teaspoon peeled and finely chopped garlic

Flour the veal slices thoroughly, shake off any excess, and brown them well in 2 tablespoons of the butter and 1 tablespoon of the oil over medium heat. Using another wide, shallow, heavy pan, brown the onion in the remaining 2 tablespoons butter and 1 tablespoon oil. Arrange the browned meat in the pan of onion without crowding, so the marrow will not fall out as the meat cooks. Cook for a couple of minutes, then add the wine and simmer.

When the wine has partially evaporated, add enough stock or water to bring the sauce near the top without covering the meat entirely. Season with salt and pepper. Cook, covered, for 1½ to 2 hours over low heat, until the meat is very tender, adding broth or water as necessary to maintain enough sauce. Stir and baste occasionally while cooking, and make sure that the meat does not stick to the pan.

The sauce should be thick by the time the meat is finished. If it is too thin, remove the veal from the pan, turn up the heat, and reduce the sauce until thick. Then return the meat to the pan.

To make the *gremolada,* mix the parsley, grated lemon peel, and chopped garlic together. Sprinkle some on each piece of meat, and let it cook a few minutes longer. Serve with *risotto alla milanese.*
(Photographs left and opposite page)

Cooked ossobuco *(recipe above right) with* risotto alla milanese *(recipe page 79) at the Ristorante Pierino in Viganò.*

OPPOSITE ▶

Ingredients for ossobuco *(recipe above) and* risotto alla milanese *(recipe page 79), at Pier Giuseppe Penati's Ristorante Pierino in Viganò.*

The literal translation for the name of the following dish could be "cod in the pot," since cassoeula *means* casseruola, *or "pot." This dish is typical of the Lodigano area.*

Practically every Italian region has its own salt cod dish. This one is distinguished by its mild flavor. If possible, use cod that has already been soaked and washed by your fishmonger. (Numerous delicatessen stores in Northern Italy soak salt cod daily in winter so it is readily available for cooking.) Serve as a main course with fried or grilled polenta (recipe page 25) on the side.

Merluzzo in Cassoeula   Stewed Codfish

From Franco Colombani of the Albergo del Sole, Maleo

Serves 6

The finished result for merluzzo in cassoeula *at the Albergo del Sole (recipe left).*

1½ pounds salt cod, rinsed and
   soaked in water overnight
½ cup flour
¼ cup plus 2 tablespoons olive oil
2 cups milk
1 cup peeled and finely chopped
   onion

2 tablespoons butter
¾ cup coarsely chopped canned
   plum tomatoes with their juice
Freshly ground pepper to taste

Wash and dry the pieces of codfish. Dust them with flour on both sides. Sauté the pieces in ¼ cup olive oil over medium heat, turning them when the first side is golden brown. When both sides are browned, remove and drain on paper towels. When cooled a bit, break the fish up into chunks, and let soak in the milk.

Sauté the onion in 2 tablespoons olive oil and the butter until limp, then add the tomatoes and their juice. When the onions are thoroughly cooked, add the codfish and all the milk and cook for about another 10 minutes. Season with freshly ground pepper.

While the fish is cooking, grill or fry slices of polenta. When the fish is done, season it with more pepper to taste, and serve.
(Photographs above right and opposite page)

A shepherd with his flock on the road near Domodossola.

◄ OPPOSITE
Ingredients and the partial preparation for merluzzo in cassoeula *at the Albergo del Sole (recipe above).*

Two typical Lombardian cakes: on top, torta sbrisolona *(recipe bottom right) and below,* torta di tagliatelle *(recipe right), at Dal Pescatore in Canneto sull'Oglio.*

Pasta becomes a dessert in torta di tagliatelle. *This cake probably originated as a way to recycle leftover pasta to serve to children on the farm. It brings to mind the Neapolitan Easter cake* pastiera *(recipe page 193), which comes from the term* pasta di ieri, *or "yesterday's pasta."*

This cake should always be made with homemade tagliatelle, *as the recipe calls for a pasta made with unusual ingredients. Torta di tagliatelle is a specialty of the Bassa Mantovana area.*

Torta di Tagliatelle   Tagliatelle Cake

From Antonio Santini of Dal Pescatore, Canneto sull'Oglio

Serves 6

The *tagliatelle:*

3½ cups all-purpose flour
4 egg yolks
6 tablespoons vermouth
½ cup liqueur, such as Amaretto di
   Saronno, Sassolino, or Strega

The cake:

1¼ cups whole almonds
10 *amaretti* cookies
1½ cups sugar
2 teaspoons vanilla
1⅓ cups sweetened cocoa
Butter and flour to prepare the pan
4 tablespoons (½ stick) butter, cut
   in small pieces

Preheat the oven to 350°.

Prepare the *tagliatelle* following the directions on page 247, using the ingredients listed here. Knead to a firm yet soft dough. When the dough is ready, roll it up and cut it into ¼-inch strips.

For the cake, blanch the almonds in boiling water; peel and finely chop or grate them. Crush the cookies to a powder.

Mix the sugar and vanilla in a bowl, then add the cocoa, almonds, and crushed cookies. Mix together well.

Butter and flour a 10-inch springform pan. Place a layer of *tagliatelle* in the pan, then sprinkle 1 or 2 spoonsful of the macaroon/almond mixture on top, then another layer of pasta, and so on, until there are 3 or 4 layers in all. Sprinkle pieces of butter on top, and bake for about 30 minutes. Serve warm or cooled.   *(Photograph left)*

The name of this cake is in dialect, from the Italian verb sbriciolare, *which means "to crumble." It is a dry cake, difficult to cut in slices, and breaks into pieces easily.*

Torta Sbrisolona   Crumbly Cake

From Antonio Santini of Dal Pescatore, Canneto sull'Oglio

Serves 6

1½ cups whole almonds
2 cups flour
1 cup corn flour
1 cup sugar
1 teaspoon grated lemon peel

2 egg yolks
2 teaspoons vanilla
½ pound (2 sticks) butter, softened
6 tablespoons lard or Crisco
Confectioners' sugar

Preheat the oven to 350°.

Blanch the almonds in boiling water, then peel and finely chop or grate them.

Combine the almonds, flours, sugar, and grated lemon peel in a mixing bowl. Add the egg yolks and vanilla. Combine the butter with the lard or Crisco, and add to the dry ingredients. Mix until crumbly; the batter will be quite dry. Pat it into a buttered 9-inch springform pan and bake for 1 hour. Remove from the oven, cool, sprinkle with confectioners' sugar, and serve. *(Photograph opposite page)*

Lodi seems to have been the birthplace of mascarpone, *a delicious cream cheese with the consistency of soft butter.* Mascarpone *can be eaten plain, with fruit or sugar, or flavored with cocoa or coffee. It is often whipped up with liqueurs for use in desserts.*

The corn flour used in this recipe is available in most health food stores.

Sabbiosa con Crema di Mascarpone

Cake Topped with Mascarpone

From Franco Colombani of the Albergo del Sole, Maleo

Serves 6

The cake:	The topping:
2 cups sugar	5 eggs, separated
⅞ pound (3½ sticks) butter, melted	5 tablespoons sugar
3¼ cups corn flour	1 pound *mascarpone*
4 eggs	¼ cup rum or Cognac
1½ teaspoons baking powder	
½ cup Cognac	
Butter and plain dried breadcrumbs to prepare the pan	

Preheat the oven to 350°.

To prepare the cake, combine the sugar and melted butter in a bowl, then fold in the flour. Add 1 egg at a time, beating each in until the mixture is smooth. Dissolve the baking powder in the Cognac and blend it into the mixture.

Butter a 9-inch springform pan and sprinkle it with breadcrumbs, shaking off any excess. Pour in the cake mixture and bake for 55 minutes. Do not open the oven during the baking time. When it is done, remove the cake from the oven, place it on a wire rack while still in the pan, and cool to room temperature.

While the cake is cooling, make the topping. Beat the 5 egg yolks and the sugar into a smooth cream; then blend in the *mascarpone*. Whip the 5 egg whites until thick, and fold into the topping together with the rum or Cognac. Mix well and refrigerate until ready to serve.

When the cake has cooled, remove it from the pan, cut into individual slices, and serve with a dollop of the chilled topping on each slice. *(Photograph right)*

Some ingredients and the finished result for sabbiosa con crema di mascarpone *at the Albergo del Sole in Maleo (recipe left).*

Spumanti grapes used in making the prized aceto balsamico.

Pere al Forno Baked Pears

From Chef Fulvio De Santa of the restaurant Peck, Milan

Serves 6

  6 large, firm pears, washed thoroughly
  1 cup dry Marsala wine
  1 cup sugar
  ⅔ cup water
  1 stick cinnamon

Preheat the oven to 325°.

Stand the unpeeled pears in a large baking dish. Pour the wine over the pears, sprinkle them with the sugar, then pour the water into the dish and put in the cinnamon stick. Bake for 1½ to 2 hours, until the pears are soft, basting every 20 minutes.

  Serve warm or cold, with the sauce poured over.

(Photograph opposite page)

Franco Colombani's loft for aging aceto balsamico, *balsamic vinegar. To make this vinegar, wine is put into large barrels with ferment, then stored in lofts where the water slowly evaporates, condensing the* aceto *to a thicker and thicker substance, almost like an oil. As it ages it is transferred to smaller and smaller barrels. The entire process can take more than twenty years, and the result is an extraordinarily flavorful essence used by the drop to season salads.*

OPPOSITE ▶
The ingredients and result for pere al forno, *a simple and delicious dessert prepared by Franco Colombani at the Albergo del Sole in Maleo (recipe from Peck's restaurant in Milan, above).*

IV. *Tuscany*

Iᴛ ᴛᴀᴋᴇs ᴀ ᴘᴇᴀsᴀɴᴛ, or at least a republican, to love Florence. Her most influential "nobility," the Medici, began as pharmacists; Michelangelo, most famous of her artists, was a rough, outspoken thug of a man, who slept in his boots (until they had to be cut off him) and was fond of a good brawl; her cooking is typified by a book, *Con poco o nulla (With Little or Nothing)*, which opens with ten suggestions for using day-old bread.

Florence's dislike for haute cuisine, like its aversion to admitting a fixed hierarchy, is rooted in its past as an autonomous city-state. There was no court as such, but instead, a strong tradition of public assembly, and a people less interested in princes than in football.

In keeping with Florence's egalitarian sentiments, there is no class system in the trattorias that feed the city. At their communal wooden tables, you are as likely to rub shoulders with the wealthy Frescobaldi family as with the tripe vendor. A man next to me, the kind of whom Dante wrote "he came down from Fiesole in the old time and still smacks of the mountain and the hard rock," started up a conversation one day:

"So, you are Scottish."

"Half."

"Good country, Scotland. Bad food, good whiskey. Edinburgh—*che bella città!*—beautiful and hard, just like Florence. And Scottish people, they are like us, independent, forthright. Not like those sneaky, snotty Sienese."

Siena and Florence have been adversaries since the Guelph and Ghibelline wars in medieval times. Florence was Guelph, for commerce and the Pope. Siena was Ghibelline, feudal, pro-Emperor. Florence's brooding, solid Renaissance palaces are gray Pietra Serena stone from the quarries of Maiano, with an almost Presbyterian distaste for ornament. This is, above all, a muscular, austere, unpretty sort of place, a bachelor's town. Its rival's Gothic towers are burnished, glowing "burnt Siena," lit by the Age of Chivalry's dying fires, as is its perilous horse race, the Palio; Siena is a city of aristocrats.

While Florence's painters discovered volume and, with Masaccio, gave Adam the muscles of a Tuscan laborer, her cooks filled bellies with *bistecche alla fiorentina*—steaks the size of tabletops. The Sienese ignored the Renaissance and kept to old Byzantine stylization. And they preferred ancient cakes, *panforte, cantucci, ricciarelli,* made with spices and ground almonds from the East.

Any chapter on Tuscany must begin with Florence. With the exception of Lucca (which retained its independence until Napoleon's time), all other Tuscan city-states—Pisa, Siena, Arezzo—fell to Florence one by one. For six hundred years or more, the city has ruled the region's politics, its art, its culture, and its cuisine.

ᴏᴘᴘᴏsɪᴛᴇ▶

Arista di maiale arrosto con fagioli all'olio, *roast pork and beans, at the Cave di Maiano near Fiesole (recipe page 106, with a similar recipe for beans to be served with the pork).*

◀ᴏᴠᴇʀʟᴇᴀғ

Sunset over the Ponte Vecchio in Florence, viewed from the Piazzale Michelangiolo above the city.

Ingredients and the finished result for panzanella, *a tomato and bread salad served as an antipasto at the Locanda dell'Amorosa, near Sinalunga (recipe page 102).*

Tuscany tastes of Florentine frugality, a trait which outlasted the extravagance of the Medici family. In the fifteenth century there existed sumptuary legislation, forbidding ostentatious dinner parties of more than three courses, a law the Medici ingeniously evaded by putting both meat and sweet in the same dish. Their chefs created vast *torte* of pastry filled with fried chicken, *ravioli*, ham, sausages, all layered with dates and almonds. For one eighty-five-dish banquet in honor of the marriage of Henry IV of France to Marie de' Medici, the sculptor Giambologna was commissioned to model elaborate statues in sugar. Such a public display of wealth seems to contradict Florence's reputation, but even the Medici had simple, private tastes, as indicated in a letter from Piero, Lorenzo de' Medici's son, to his father: "Please send me some figs, for I like them. I mean those red ones, and some peaches with stones, and other things you know I like. . . ."

A preference for good ingredients over elaborate sauces is typical of Tuscany, where the favorite sauce is a thread of extra virgin, vivid green olive oil. The olives should be underripe, for the most piquancy, and picked by hand to avoid bruising, the cause of oxidation and acidity.

Olive oil is the base of the Tuscan culinary pyramid, for it is the frying medium of *soffritto*, the mixture of finely chopped aromatics which is the prelude to all savory dishes. Tuscan soups are given a last-minute "blessing" of oil, and oil bastes Tuscan roasts and fennel sausages (*finocchione*) and is simmered with dried beans to soften them, then added, raw, as a peppery dressing (recipe page 106).

Tuscans claim their oil is the best in Italy, and its bold fruitiness is certainly best with their *piattellini* beans (less starchy than *cannellini*). Quality and flavor vary, however, depending on where the trees are grown. Oils from Lucca are delicate and golden, ideal with fish, as they are from the southern coast, where the delicacy has a hint of pepper. Those from the steep Chianti hills and the Valdarno are dark, fuller-bodied, intense.

The finest oil, *di prima spremitura extra vergine* (extra virgin, first pressed within a few days of picking), has one-half to one percent acidity, a level which rises to about four percent as quality decreases. Genuine Tuscan oil should have *prodotto e imbottigliato* (produced and bottled) or "estate bottled" on the label. This ensures that the olives were not brought in from another region, a deception common after the bitter winter of 1984–85, which decimated thousands of Tuscan olive trees—while mysteriously failing to decimate the quantity of expensive "Tuscan" olive oil. An olive tree can regenerate itself from an under-

Tuscan flavors in the kitchen of Lorenza de' Medici at Badia a Coltibuono: hot-pepper-flavored olive oil, flowering sage, rosemary, and dried fennel.

Spiedini, a classic Tuscan dish of sausages and liver wrapped in pig's intestines and grilled with bread, bay leaves, and wild fennel, at Badia a Coltibuono in Chianti.

7

6

5

3

2

1

4

8

ground stump, but it takes a good five years before it grows into a bush with sufficient fruit to produce oil.

After olive oil, herbs are the most important ingredients in Tuscan cooking—nowhere else in Italy are they so widely used. And rosemary, along with the smoke from a chestnut wood fire, is the smell most evocative of Tuscan kitchens. Dipped in olive oil, the herb is used to baste roast pork and lamb (recipes for roasted meats with rosemary, pages 104 and 106), and its toughest branches are threaded with sausages and caul-wrapped liver for *spiedini* (skewers) to be grilled over wood embers. *Pan di ramerino*, a sweet roll mentioned by the fourteenth-century Merchant of Prato, is no more than dough enriched with extra sugar and heavily scented with rosemary leaves.

In the Chianti region I had a lesson in more unusual flavorings from an herbalist and vinegar maker named Dado, a born-again peasant.

"My mother, who was a real city woman, told me that all her life she had looked at grass and seen nothing more than grass. Then one day during the war, when we were sent away to the country, she saw that in one square meter of grass there were fifty other plants struggling to exist. It seems to me to say something about life as well as grass."

"It's the romance of herbalism, then, that appeals to you."

"It's the taste!" he said.

He knew the difference between stewing herbs, to be served with olive oil and lemon, such as mallow, wild leeks, clary, and radicchio; and those less bitter, destined for salad, which include the pretty, serrated leaves of salad burnet.

"There is an old saying here," he told me. "*L'insalata non è bella se non c'è la salvastrella*—which means that a salad is not beautiful without salad burnet."

Tuscan peasants, he said, who had known in the past how to prepare some two thousand different wild herbs and weeds, were losing their knowledge. Only city people were still attracted by country ways. "When the man who helps with my vines sees me picking wild chicory to boil and eat with oil and *pecorino*, he says, 'Oh yes, I remember my grandmother doing that.' But he has broken from his past like a train from its engine."

One problem has been the demise of the ancient Tuscan sharecropping system, the *mezzadria*, by which a group of farmers shared profits with a wealthy proprietor, and lived around his villa in great families or farms. Although the farmers' share had risen to half by the end of the *mezzadria* in the 1960s, they had begun to abandon the land much earlier, when they discovered more money could be made in the city.

"The city was like a mirage for them," said Dado.

Landowners who could not match city wages were forced to enlarge fields to accommodate machinery, or to sell off property. Luckily, many of the new owners were interested in preserving the old working landscape of vineyards and olive trees, but some of the most beautiful parts of Tuscany now have telephone books with more foreign than Italian names.

Not all the changes of modern times are for the worst, however. Tourism has brought increased prosperity to poor families in the Apennine mountains of northwest Tuscany, whose diet used to consist of

1. *View inside the walled town of San Gimignano.*

2. *In the cellars of the Enoteca Pinchiorri, a famous wine shop and restaurant in Florence.*

3. *The garden at Badia a Coltibuono in Chianti.*

4. *A pigeon drinking from a fountain in the Piazza del Campo in Siena.*

5. *Miranda Minucci in her grocery store, La Villa Miranda, next door to her restaurant near Radda in Chianti.*

6. *A view of Monteriggioni, a thirteenth-century walled village.*

7. *Old copper cooking utensils in the kitchen at Badia a Coltibuono.*

8. *A hot tripe sandwich stand in the streets of Florence.*

weeds and chestnuts and whatever game they could kill. The damp, sweet chestnut flour ground at water-powered mills has always been used by the poor to make breads and rustic Tuscan desserts. Now it has become fashionable, no bad thing for those who produce it.

The Maremma (meaning coastal plain), in southwest Tuscany, a malaria-ridden swamp until less than a century ago, has been cleared and turned into fertile meadows that nourish herds of cattle rivaling Chianti's white Chianina (the best beef in Italy, essential for classic *bistecca alla fiorentina*). Here one still finds culinary echoes of those "long-nosed, subtly-smiling Etruscans" so admired by D. H. Lawrence, and of medieval cooks, whose sweet-and-sour sauces such as *agrodolce*, of sugar, vinegar, pine nuts, and candied fruit, are used to sauce the wild boar common in the region.

Sheep as well as cattle graze the rolling Maremma plains and produce milk for Tuscan *pecorino* cheese. In April and May you will see fresh young *marzolino*, "little spring" *pecorino*, being eaten with raw

Farm scenery near San Quirico. This kind of undisturbed pastoral scene is increasingly difficult to find in Tuscany, and throughout Italy as well.

fava beans *(bacelli)* and a crude dip of olive oil and salt; the summer cheese, ripened now and rubbed with tomato or ashes while aging, is eaten with firm sweet pears. These dishes, two of the purest and most Tuscan, are available in all good country-style trattorias—but never on their menus.

Like icebergs, Tuscan menus conceal more than they reveal. I remember arriving late at a small place in Lucca to be told that there was no food left.

"Not even some bread?" Bread, yes. "And perhaps some *salame?*" Well, if the *signorina* did not mind wild boar sausage. "No cheese?" If she could bear old *pecorino* and a few *bacelli* . . . and there might be one last slice of the *torta di verdure* (a local sweet tart made with Swiss chard and candied fruit).

None of these things was on the menu.

"But if the *signorina* had told us she only wanted bread and a snack—we thought she wanted *food!*"

Bread, the classic, saltless *pan sciocco,* is the pasta of Tuscany. With the exception of three-quarter-inch-wide *pappardelle* noodles and the eggless, snaky *pici* made around Siena, pasta is of negligible importance here. Day-old bread, on the other hand, is the foundation of recipes from *acquacotta* (cooked water)—bread covered in water that has been boiled with garlic and herbs, sometimes with an egg poached in it—to *panzanella*, a salad of wet bread, tomatoes, onions, basil, and olive oil (recipe page 102). And once-risen bread dough, dredged with icing sugar, or enriched with such things as honey or candied fruit, is often the point of departure for Tuscan desserts. Rolled out flat and studded with wine grapes at harvest time, it becomes the Chiantigiana's favorite tart, *schiacciata con l'uva* (recipe page 109).

More complicated dishes do exist: Renaissance cooks picked up recipes for béchamel and mayonnaise from French chefs (and taught them about pastry and ice cream); Florence's restaurants are more nouvelle than they once were. Yet the art of Tuscan cuisine remains that of subtraction rather than addition. Perfectly spit-roasted game, creamy beans simmered in a Chianti flask: these dishes may seem plain to the point of nonexistence, but their very simplicity makes them difficult to reproduce.

I am reminded of Giotto, who, when asked by his pope to submit samples of work, simply drew a perfect freehand circle in red chalk and sent it along. A typically Florentine gesture—the confidence of a man who knows the value of his product.

Seeing Tuscany for the first time—those olive groves and cypresses and vine-striped hills blurred by quattrocento light—one recognizes it from a thousand paintings. Wine has always been a part of this landscape. There have been vineyards on these hills since Etruscan times, and by the thirteenth century the Chianti region's feudal barons had formed probably the world's first wine consortium. More recently, the barons and their competitors have been at the center of a wine revolution.

Tuscany was ruled in the past by a red grape, Sangiovese, affectionately known as "Giovetto," and by its three most famous offspring: Chianti (the largest DOC district in Italy, both in territory and volume of wine); Brunello di Montalcino (at its best, a rich and meaty wine with extraordinary longevity; one of the world's priciest); and Vino Nobile di Montepulciano (a longer-aged version of Chianti whose reputation as "king" of wines is often unjustified).

Shouldering this establishment aside are modern wines whose producers—some of the oldest names in the business—have revolted against restrictive DOC regulations (equivalent to France's *appellation contrôlée*). They are planting French grapes where Italian varieties once grew, blending Sangiovese with Merlot or with Cabernet Sauvignon, and aging the product in small French oak casks, usually new, rather than in the huge old casks of the past. By breaking the rules, they forfeit DOC and must settle for *vino da tavola* status, once a sign of a very ordinary wine. The irony is that these *vino da tavola* wines are often more expensive and more exciting than their DOC neighbors.

It would be impossible to list all the excellent newcomers. One key is to look for producers who have already established good names in old-style Tuscan wines (Castello di Volpaia, for example, produces one of the best Chiantis as well as some of the most innovative modern blends—as do Antinori, Frescobaldi, Villa Banfi, and Barbi Colombini), and to remember that these traditional wines are constantly having their blends and vinification techniques improved as well.

There are drawbacks. While small French barrels give a quick return in oaky taste, they also exaggerate a wine's potential, disastrous if that potential is not there. The inferior white Trebbiano grape, part of the old Chianti cocktail being dropped by modern producers, is no great loss (in a blind tasting you could mistake it for water). However, too great an enthusiasm for French grapes and techniques could result in a tragic loss of Tuscan flavor.

Leslie Forbes

OPPOSITE
Torta di lamponi, *raspberry tart, and* torta di fichi, *fig tart, served at the Cave di Maiano, near Fiesole outside of Florence.*

This is one of many traditional bread-based dishes that were once a staple of peasant fare, and are now increasingly difficult to find in restaurants. Other bread dishes include panzanella *(a bread and tomato salad, recipe page 102); and* acquacotta, *literally "cooked water," from the Maremma area.* Pappa al pomodoro *is said to be delicious even a few days after it has been made.*

Pappa al Pomodoro   Tomato and Bread Soup

From Lorenza de' Medici at Badia a Coltibuono, near Gaiole

Serves 4

⅓ cup olive oil, plus extra for
   garnish
3 teaspoons peeled and finely
   chopped garlic
3 cups seeded and chopped fresh
   tomatoes
1 tablespoon rinsed and chopped
   fresh basil leaves

5 cups meat stock
Salt and pepper to taste
12 cups ½-inch bread cubes made
   from very stale whole wheat bread
Freshly grated Parmigiano cheese
   to taste

Some ingredients and the finished result for pappa al pomodoro *at Badia a Coltibuono (recipe left).*

Heat ⅓ cup oil in a deep pot and sauté the garlic, then add the tomatoes and basil and cook for 5 to 10 minutes. Add the stock, season with salt and pepper, and continue to heat. When the soup starts boiling, add the stale bread pieces, and cook, stirring, for another few minutes. Then cover the pot and leave to simmer for 1 hour.

When the soup is done, pour some fresh olive oil on it and serve hot, warm, or cold with Parmigiano cheese.   *(Photograph above right)*

◄ OPPOSITE PAGE
The ingredients for making tagliatelle alla maggiorana *at the Locanda dell'Amorosa, near Sinalunga (recipe below left).*

Tagliatelle alla Maggiorana

Marjoram-flavored Tagliatelle

From Carlo Citterio of the Locanda dell'Amorosa, near Sinalunga

Serves 6

The pasta:
2¼ cups flour
3 eggs
1 teaspoon chopped fresh marjoram,
   or ⅓ teaspoon dried marjoram
1 teaspoon salt

The sauce:
¼ cup ground walnuts
2 tablespoons ground pine nuts
6 tablespoons (¾ stick) butter
¼ cup freshly grated Parmigiano
   cheese

Make the pasta dough with the ingredients listed here following the directions for pasta on page 247, adding the chopped marjoram to the flour at the same time as the eggs (fresh marjoram is important to this recipe, and is highly recommended). After cutting, spread out the *tagliatelle* on a floured dishcloth so that they do not stick together.

To make the sauce, toast the ground nuts in a baking pan in a 250° oven, keeping an eye on them so they do not burn. Melt the butter in a large pan and add the toasted nuts. Cook the pasta in plenty of boiling salted water for a minute or 2, drain it well, put it into the butter/nut sauce, and toss together. Sprinkle the Parmigiano cheese on top and serve immediately.
(Photographs right and opposite page)

Tagliatelle alla maggiorana, *just cut and drying at the Locanda dell'Amorosa (see recipe for serving this* tagliatelle, *left).*

Panzanella   Country-style Bread Salad

From Carlo Citterio of the Locanda dell'Amorosa, near Sinalunga

Serves 6

2½ stale 8-ounce loaves Italian or
  French bread
4 cups seeded and chopped fresh
  tomatoes
1½ cups trimmed, partially peeled,
  and chopped cucumber
1 serrano chile pepper, seeded and
  cut into thin strips
1 cup trimmed and chopped celery
1 medium red onion, peeled and
  thinly sliced

2 tablespoons rinsed and chopped
  fresh basil leaves
4 anchovy fillets packed in oil,
  chopped (optional)
2 hard-boiled eggs, chopped
  (optional)
1 teaspoon peeled and finely
  chopped garlic (optional)
½ cup extra virgin olive oil, plus
  extra for garnish
Salt and pepper to taste
Red wine vinegar to taste

Soak the bread in cold water for 20 minutes. Squeeze the water out firmly with your hands and crumble the bread into a salad bowl. Add all the vegetables, and any optional ingredients desired, and mix together well.

In a separate bowl, beat ½ cup olive oil with the salt and pepper. Season the salad with this simple dressing, mixing it thoroughly. Chill for at least an hour; before serving, toss the salad again, adding the vinegar and some fresh oil if desired.   *(Photograph page 92)*

Coniglio in Casseruola nel Peperone

Rabbit-stuffed Peppers

From Carlo Citterio of the Locanda dell'Amorosa, near Sinalunga

Serves 4

4 medium red or yellow sweet
  peppers
½ pound *prataioli* mushrooms, or
  domestic button mushrooms
1½ pounds boneless rabbit meat,
  cut into small pieces
2 tablespoons olive oil

½ cup dry white wine
½ cup chicken stock
½ cup chopped canned plum
  tomatoes with their juice
1 tablespoon tomato paste
Salt and pepper to taste

Preheat the oven to 400°.
Wash the peppers and cut off their tops, saving the tops for lids. Clean out the seeds and veins, but leave the peppers whole. Bake them for about 15 minutes, until they are tender but not too soft.

Wash, dry, and slice the mushrooms. Sauté the rabbit meat in a frying pan with the olive oil until it is cooked through. Drain the fat from the pan, then add the mushrooms and the wine, and simmer until the wine evaporates. Add the stock, tomatoes, and tomato paste, season with salt and pepper, and cook over low heat for 10 minutes.

Stand the peppers in an oiled baking pan just large enough to hold them, so they do not tip over. Fill them with the rabbit and mushroom mixture. Reduce the oven temperature to 350°. Cover the peppers with their lids and return them to the oven for 10 or 15 minutes, or until they are soft. Serve hot.
(Photograph 4, opposite page)

1. *People eating gelato in the street in Florence.*

2. *Breads at Il Fornaio shop in Florence.*

3. *The arrival of fresh market produce at the Locanda dell'Amorosa, near Sinalunga.*

4. *Cooked coniglio in casseruola nel peperone at the Locanda dell'Amorosa (recipe bottom left).*

5. *A typical Tuscan street scene, this one in Florence.*

6. *Various cakes and biscotti, including a package of the famous panforte Nannini di Siena.*

7. *Various gelati in Nannini's gelateria, the Italian equivalent of an ice-cream parlor, in Siena.*

8. *Little take-out pizzas for sale at Il Fornaio shop in Florence, with various toppings of local vegetables.*

9. *Torre di Pulcinella, the Clown Tower, in the old city of Montepulciano.*

1

2

3

4

5

6

7

8

9

Pollo arrosto *at the Cave di Maiano in Fiesole (recipe right).*

Pollo Arrosto   Roast Chicken

From Aldo Landi of the Cave di Maiano, near Fiesole

Serves 4

One 3-pound chicken, cut into joints	Salt and pepper to taste
6 tablespoons olive oil	1 lemon, cut into wedges
2 tablespoons fresh lemon juice	
2 teaspoons chopped fresh rosemary, or ½ teaspoon dried rosemary	

Wash the chicken thoroughly and wipe dry with paper towels. In a large, shallow bowl marinate the chicken pieces with 5 tablespoons olive oil, the lemon juice, rosemary, and salt and pepper for 1 hour. Turn the chicken pieces occasionally in the marinade.

Preheat the oven to 400°.

Heat 1 tablespoon olive oil in a large frying pan over high heat and cook the chicken pieces in the oil until they are browned on all sides.

Put the chicken pieces in a roasting pan and roast them for 10 to 12 minutes. To test if they are ready, prick one piece slightly with a knife. When the juices run clear, the chicken is done.

Remove from the oven, season again with salt and pepper, and serve the chicken garnished with lemon wedges.   *(Photograph left)*

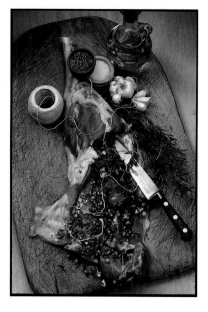

The spicing of agnello arrosto *before cooking at the Cave di Maiano (recipe right).*

Agnello Arrosto   Roast Lamb

From Aldo Landi of the Cave di Maiano, near Fiesole

Serves 6

One 3-pound leg of lamb, boned before weighing, prepared by your butcher	2 teaspoons chopped fresh rosemary, or ½ teaspoon dried rosemary
2 teaspoons peeled and chopped garlic	¼ cup olive oil
	Salt and pepper to taste
	1 cup white wine

Preheat the oven to 475°.

Lay the leg of lamb out flat and sprinkle the inside with the garlic and rosemary, 2 tablespoons of the oil, and the salt and pepper. Roll up the lamb and tie it with string.

Reduce the oven temperature to 450°. Place the meat in a roasting pan with the rest of the oil. Turn the leg to coat with the oil, pour in the wine, and roast for about 15 minutes. Then turn down the temperature again, to 400°, and roast for another hour, basting occasionally. For well-done meat, cook an additional 15 minutes. Carve in thick slices and serve with the juices, strained of fat.   *(Photographs left and opposite page)*

OPPOSITE▶
Agnello arrosto *(recipe above) with* arista di maiale arrosto *(recipe page 106), at Aldo Landi's Cave di Maiano in Fiesole.*

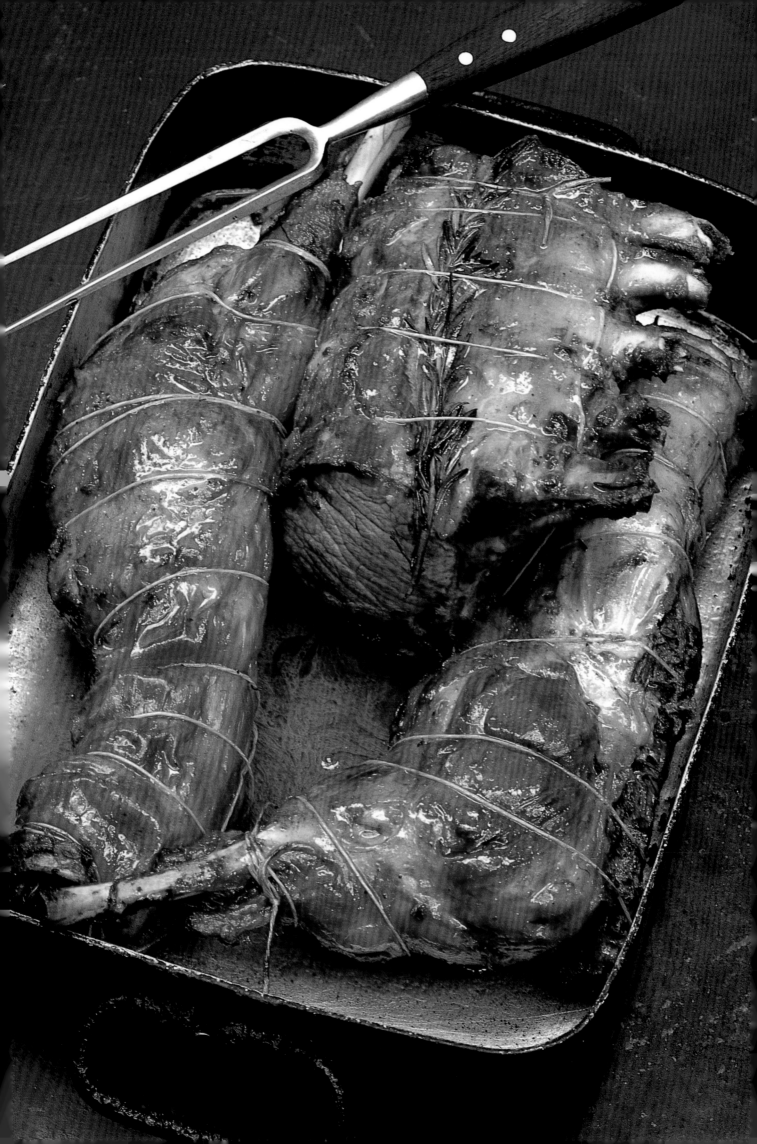

Cannellini *beans soaking before cooking, at the Locanda dell'Amorosa (recipe for cooking* cannellini *beans, below right).*

In Florence, and Tuscany in general, arista *refers to the pig's loin with ribs still attached, cut as a single piece. The origin of the name traces back to an important event in the history of the city.*

During the Seventeenth Ecumenical Council of Basel and Ferrara-Florence (1431-45), which resulted in the short-lived Union of Florence between the Roman Catholic and Eastern Orthodox churches, sumptuous banquets were offered. At one of these feasts, a joint of roast pork was served to the Greek bishops. To express their enthusiastic approval of the dish, they exclaimed, "Aristos, aristos!" meaning "Good, very good!"

Fagioli all'uccelletto (recipe below) are commonly served as a side dish to this roast pork.

Arista di Maiale Arrosto   Roast Pork Loin

From Aldo Landi of the Cave di Maiano, near Fiesole

Serves 4

2 pounds loin of pork with ribs, prepared for cooking by your butcher	2 teaspoons chopped fresh rosemary, or ½ teaspoon dried rosemary
3 teaspoons peeled and sliced garlic	Salt and pepper to taste
	2 tablespoons olive oil

Preheat the oven to 425°.

Stud the loin with garlic and rosemary (rub in dried rosemary if you are using it). Rub the loin with salt and pepper, coat with 1 tablespoon olive oil, and place the meat in a roasting pan, pouring the rest of the oil over the meat in the pan.

Roast the meat uncovered for about 15 minutes, or until it has browned nicely all over. Lower the temperature to 375° and bake for another 45 minutes, turning the meat and basting it occasionally. When the meat is done (it should be tender and moist), cool briefly, slice thinly, and serve with its juice. (*Photographs pages 91 and 105*)

The name of this dish means "beans like a bird," as the seasoning is supposed to make the fagioli *taste like small game animals. It is one of Tuscany's most famous dishes. The secret to this version lies in the careful preparation of the dried beans. The* fagioli *are recommended as an accompaniment to boiled and roasted meats, like the preceding recipes (above, and page 104).*

Fagioli all'Uccelletto   Beans in Tomato Sauce

From Aldo Landi of the Cave di Maiano, near Fiesole

Serves 4

2 cups dry *cannellini* beans	Salt to taste
4 cloves garlic, peeled	1 tablespoon olive oil
2 medium stalks celery	Freshly ground pepper to taste (optional)
2 fresh sage leaves, or ¼ teaspoon dried sage	2 cups seeded and roughly chopped fresh tomatoes
1 medium carrot, peeled	
1 medium onion, peeled	

Put the beans on the stove, preferably in an earthenware pot, with enough cold water to come 1 inch above the level of the beans. Add 3 garlic cloves, the celery stalks, 1 sage leaf (or ⅛ teaspoon dried sage), the carrot, and the onion. Place another pan of the same diameter over this pot, and fill it with a good amount of water. Cook the beans for about 2½ hours over low heat, taking care that they simmer very gently all the while. Add the warmed water in the top pan to the beans in the bottom pan as they dry out. The beans are done when they begin to be slightly mashed. Add salt only during the last 15 minutes of cooking. When the beans are done, drain them and remove the vegetables.

Heat the oil with the remaining garlic clove and sage leaf (or the remaining dried sage), both chopped, in a large pan. Add the beans, more salt if needed, and some pepper if desired. Cook the beans for a while, tossing the pan or stirring now and then so the beans don't stick to the bottom. Add the tomatoes and continue to cook for about 15 minutes. Salt, pepper, and olive oil to taste can be added right before serving.

(Photograph of a similar preparation for beans, opposite page)

An artist painting in the Piazza della Signoria in Florence.

San Gimignano lit up in the evening.

This grape bread has been made during the wine harvest for over two thousand years, since Etruscan times. The recipe comes from Lorenza de' Medici, a descendant of the legendary Medici family who ruled Tuscany during the Renaissance. Vin Santo, "holy wine," has a distinctive aromatic bouquet. It is rich and smooth, more like a sherry than a wine. It is aged in lofts in very small barrels, called caratelli. It is used here to soak the raisins, but is also recommended as an accompaniment.

Schiacciata con l'Uva   Grape Bread

From Lorenza de' Medici at Badia a Coltibuono, near Gaiole

Serves 6 to 8

2 cakes fresh yeast, or 2 packages active dry yeast	Butter or oil to prepare the pan
¾ cup warm milk	1 pound black pitted or seedless grapes, cut in halves
3¼ cups all-purpose flour	½ cup chopped walnuts
1 cup sugar	½ cup raisins soaked in Vin Santo
Pinch of salt	or a sweet dessert wine

Dissolve the yeast in the warm milk for 10 minutes. Place the flour in a large bowl and form a well in the center. Stir in the milk/yeast mixture, add ¾ cup sugar and the salt, and knead well. Leave the dough to rest in a clean cloth in a warm place until the dough doubles in size (about 2 hours).

Roll the dough out into 2 rounds, each about 12 inches in diameter. Place 1 round in a buttered or oiled baking pan large enough to hold it. Cover it with half the grapes, walnuts, and drained raisins. Cover with the second round of dough, and then the rest of the grapes, walnuts, and raisins. Sprinkle the remaining ¼ cup sugar on top. Cover the bread with a dishcloth and leave it to rise again until doubled in size.

Preheat the oven to 350°. Bake the bread for 1 hour. Serve warm or cool. *(Photograph opposite page)*

Barrels of Chianti Classico produced at Badia a Coltibuono by Lorenza de' Medici's husband, Piero Stucchi-Prinetti.

◀ OPPOSITE
Some ingredients and the finished result for schiacciata con l'uva *at Badia a Coltibuono (recipe above).*

Farmworkers along the Po valley in the 1950s.

Culatello, *cured rump of pork, being strung fresh, and cut dried, at the Terzi Vezio Stagionatura Salumi in Collecchio. Commercially produced* culatello *is cured and matured by a method similar to that used for* prosciutto di Parma, *and is delicious and expensive.*

Resident at a pig farm in Rubbiano di Solignano, at the Caseificio Rastelli, a cheese factory. The happy pigs are fed buttermilk left over from the making of Parmigiano cheese.

◄ OVERLEAF
A typical scene of Emilia-Romagna: long, straight rows of poplars by a field of sunflowers, near Volano.

V. *Emilia-Romagna*

THE LANDSCAPE OF EMILIA-ROMAGNA is dominated by a long sweep of contoured plain. Decidedly monotonous when viewed in passing from the window of a car or train, this terrain discloses to its inhabitants a seasonal drama. It begins in winter, when temperatures sink below zero, and a soupy fog seals the stubbled flats. In spring, the mists disperse, and one can make out a scroll of acreage covered with a level script of furrows and marked off by straight margins of poplars. In summer, the muted tones are brightened by a patch of poppies, ecstatically red, and a wide sea of sunflowers. In autumn, the land is lushly quilted with crops: a tractor emerges from a stone shed, turns onto a dirt road, and makes its way to a wheat field. At the top of a rise, a few human forms bend devotionally over their plantings, inspecting the harvest.

The hinterlands of Emilia-Romagna preserve the ancient ideal of servitude to the land. It is not a punishing servitude. This broad reach of soil, watered and fed by the Po River and its tributaries, Alpine and Apennine, is as fertile as any in Italy, and amply rewards those who cultivate it. A fifth of the nation's wheat grows here, and half its sugar beet, along with a profusion of fruits and vegetables—apples, cherries, strawberries, watermelon; artichokes, potatoes, asparagus, zucchini, many varieties of *porcini* mushrooms. Rice crops cover the marshy stretch near the banks of the Po, whose crooked course traces the region's northern border.

Much of the bounty goes to the canneries, mills, and processing plants clumped at intervals along the Via Emilia, a busy *autostrada* one hundred and fifty miles long. What is not exported from this land is transformed—into splendid dishes. Emilia-Romagna, long Italy's leader in food production, is also its gastronomic capital.

It is a cuisine marked by richness, refinement, and subtlety, distinctly Old World. Recipes here use butter and lard, rather than oil—olive groves, once abundant, were cleared, centuries ago, to make way for more lucrative crops. A sideboard typically is laden with meat: veal, pork, and sausage. Purposeful gastronomes can flush out more exotic fare—guinea hen, pheasant, woodcock, even wild boar—all favorites, centuries ago, of the local nobility, who stocked the surrounding hillsides with game. Today the legacy is popularly preserved in *bollito misto,* an assortment of boiled meats served on occasions when no fewer than fifteen guests gather at table (recipe page 130).

Other meats, prepared in smaller quantities, are closely identified with a specific city. The list is headed by *prosciutto di Parma* (Parma ham)—Italy's premier antipasto, pink and sweet, best when sliced paper thin. Bologna's pride is *costoletta alla bolognese,* a veal cutlet stuffed with cheese and truffle, and then breaded—or surmounted with a layer of ham and cheese. In the windows of Modena's butcher shops hang rows of *zampone,* pig's trotter cleaned of all bone and cartilage, and then crammed to the toes with seasoned pork forcemeat. First boiled, *zampone* is served with any one of several relishes, each flavored with a dash of another Modenese specialty, *aceto balsamico* (balsamic vinegar). Ferrara's *salame da sugo* is a garlicky mixture of minced pork, liver, and tongue. *Culatello,* made from choice pork rump, is the specialty in Busseto, a hamlet on the border of Lombardy where Giuseppe Verdi, born a few kilometers away in Roncoli, liked to dine.

No less varied is this region's range of pastas, which come in different shapes, sizes, and even shadings (green, if made with spinach or nettle juice), and which are often filled. Bologna's *tortellini* are said to have been created by a cook who envisioned the navel of an adored woman as he wound the first noodle around his pinky. Bolognesi serve *tortellini* with *ragù* (meat sauce, recipe page 124) or *in brodo* (in beef or chicken broth). Parma's *tortelli alle erbette* has a creamy filling of ricotta blended with beet, spinach, and sometimes Swiss chard (recipe page 123). Ricotta is used as well in Piacenza's *tortelli alla piacentina*. In this region with its many pig farms, pasta sauces are commonly flavored with *pancetta*, an unsmoked bacon. At table, diners dust their helpings with *parmigiano-reggiano* cheese, so treasured that each of two cities—Parma and Reggio—lays unique claim to it.

All these dishes originated in Emilia, which makes up roughly two-thirds of the region, its western portion, extending from Bologna to Piacenza. The area's name derives from the Via Emilia, completed in 187 B.C. as a vital segment in the system of highways that connected ancient Rome to its distant colonies. Today the route is overlaid by the high-speed *autostrada,* which shuttles traffic the entire length of the region, passing through cities that in the Middle Ages and Renaissance were among the most important in all of Europe, and that now rank among Italy's wealthiest: Bologna, Modena, Parma, Reggio nell'Emilia.

In the north, three miles from the banks of the Po and the Veneto border, sits Ferrara, "the first modern city in Europe," Jacob Burckhardt declared in *Civilization of the Renaissance in Italy.* Ferrara was a key outpost of the Papal States governed by the imperious Este clan. The Castello Estense, begun in 1385 after an uprising by overtaxed citizens, still looks girded for assault, with its four commanding towers and emphatic moat. The idea was to keep marauders out and potential escapees in—the Estes played rough. Lucrezia Borgia, brought into the family by marriage (and a huge dowry), was a mere *innocente* compared to, say, Niccolò III, who, suspecting a dalliance between his wife and his son, calmly beheaded both. Now he smirks at posterity from atop a pedestal in the Palazzo del Comune. The last of the ducal line, Alfonso II, much admired for his punctilio, inspired, long after his death, Robert Browning's chilling poem "My Last Duchess," whose narrator reports the unfortunate end met by his bride because she had "A heart—how shall I say?—too soon made glad." Greater warmth radiates from Ferrara's current inhabitants. The *padrone* at our *pensione* amused us with a spirited discourse on the enigma of New York's Italian-Americans ("John Gotti and Mario Cuomo, the worst and the best, in the same city!").

With it all, the Estes were a civic-minded clan, who gave their subjects wide, level boulevards and a municipal park, one of Europe's first. In the twentieth century, Giorgio de Chirico painted for some years in Ferrara. His "metaphysical" canvases refract the city's mad scramble of incongruous forms, like the arcade of commercial shops tucked into one long side of the rosy cathedral.

Castello and *cattedrale* stand squarely in the middle of the old town and at evening cast deep shadows. In them Ferrarese of all ages, many on bicycles, converge for relaxed conversation. Visiting Americans marvel at the casual bridging of Italy's generations, young and old brought so easily together as if united

1. *Rows of* prosciutto *drying and aging at the Quattro Stagioni Prosciuttificio (a ham factory) in Langhirano.*

2. *Watermelon and cantaloupe in the market in Modena.*

3. *A barrel of aging* aceto balsamico *in the attic at the Fini factory in Modena. Some barrels are kept especially for family or friends, who take the vinegar a little at a time; this barrel is kept for a priest.*

4. *Fresh* paste *at the Antica Trattoria del Cacciatore in Bologna, top to bottom:* tagliatelle, tortellini, farfalline, *and* tortelli all'ortica *(recipe page 123).*

5. *Julio Monari in front of his Carducci restaurant in Modena with Lucia Zampolli, who makes the pasta for the restaurant.*

6. Taglioline, *a very fine pasta, just being cut by Wanda Ferrari at the Antica Trattoria del Cacciatore in Bologna.*

7. Crescenta *bread made with bacon chips at the Antica Trattoria del Cacciatore.*

8. *A friendly fisherman on the Po River at Lido di Guastalla, northeast of Parma. He is fishing just for fun, as pollution in the river makes his catch quite inedible.*

9. *A roadside advertisement for fresh watermelon near Cadecoppi.*

1

2

3

4

5

6

7

8

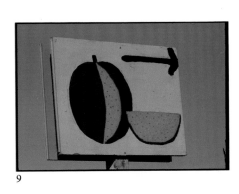

9

by the magnetizing pull of the past—or by their shared abashment, so painful has Italy's long history been. A monument in Ferrara mourns the Jews who perished in World War II, sent to Nazi death camps, a trauma described by the Ferrarese novelist Giorgio Bassani in *The Garden of the Finzi-Continis*. The legacy survives more cheerfully in the Jewish provenance of many local specialties, which replace pork with goose, chicken, and rabbit. Ferrara also features the pumpkin-filled *tortellini* now so popular in the United States (similar recipe from the Veneto on page 22), and the cap-shaped and -named *cappellacci*, and *cappelletti*.

The Estes, turning their greedy gaze southward, coveted Modena, situated amid the fruited plain. What they wanted they took: Modena was theirs from the fourteenth century to the nineteenth, and today it wears the fastidious Este stamp. It is a city of fine proportions and impressive wealth, much of it owing to Ferrari and Maserati—the auto companies have plants nearby. Gastronomes honor two other names, Fini and Federzoni, both manufacturers of *aceto balsamico*, balsamic vinegar, the dark elixir better known to Americans than to most Italians. The Modenese credit the vinegar with curative powers (hence *balsamico*). Lucrezia Borgia swore it eased the pangs of childbirth.

Modenese families produce their own *aceto,* using methods that date back centuries. Its base is Trebbiano grapes, boiled down to a must, then poured when cold into a *batteria* of barrels, no fewer than five, of descending size (from fifty liters to ten). Each barrel is made of a different wood (most often cherry, chestnut, juniper, mulberry, and oak), and has its own aroma, which seeps into the liquid as it ages. The *batteria* is locked in the family attic, the ideal venue because it is subject to the extreme temperatures the *aceto* requires. The woman of the house—it is always she who holds the key—draws the annual supply from the smallest barrel, whose contents have aged, in some instances, a hundred years (an eyeblink to the Estes, who preferred to let it sit for three centuries). Modenese sprinkle it on everything—including strawberries.

This vinegar travels better, some would say, than any of Emilia-Romagna's wines, better even than Modena's ebullient Lambrusco, a dry red, flavored with violets, altogether unlike the sweet version American importers overstocked a few fads ago. Three other wines deserve mention: Albano and Trebbiano (both whites) and Sangiovese (red). All three come from the Romagnan slopes of the Apennine range.

Fittingly, the dining capital of Emilia-Romagna is also its major city, Bologna, whose nicknames include "la Grassa" (the Fat) and "la Dotta" (the Learned). These characteristics are easily paired, for food and erudition go together here. No one was surprised when an avant-garde theater group at the august University of Bologna—the oldest in Christendom, founded in 1088—staged a production of Pellegrino Artusi's *La scienza in cucina o l'arte del mangiar bene (Science in the Kitchen or the Art of Good Eating),*

Parma hams drying the old way in the attic at the Prosciuttificio of the Fratelli Adorni Ivo e Remigio in Felino, near Parma.

A serving of Parma ham and figs at the Ristorante Da Ceci, run by the Ceci family in an eighteenth-century hunting lodge in Collecchio once owned by Napoleon's second wife, Marie Louise.

OPPOSITE▶
Parma ham and figs waiting to be cut and served at the Ristorante Da Ceci in the Villa Maria Luigia in Collecchio.

Italy's classic cookbook, first published in 1891. Artusi was the Garibaldi of *la cucina italiana*, who hoped to create a culinary *Risorgimento* based on (or biased toward) the recipes of Emilia-Romagna. His spirit survives in Bologna's chamber of commerce, where a perfectly turned *tagliatelle* is solemnly preserved.

Bologna was also for many years the Jerusalem of Eurocommunism. "You must go there," urged the fervent youths in Perugia, where I, no less fervent, was struggling to learn Italian at the Università per Stranieri. This was in 1976, the American bicentennial. It seemed a good idea to learn what the postcapitalist future held. I expected, I suppose, a proletarian Disneyland, but found instead in Bologna a medieval city with a superb enclosed square, the Piazza Maggiore, surveyed by the reddish immensity of San Petronio, a church, never completed, all the more imposing for being unfinished, as though it might suddenly take new, and even larger, shape. The old city of Bologna is ingeniously networked with porticoed streets, and I stalked them, ignoring boutiques, *salumerie,* each with a phantasmal array of sausages, multitudinous *ristoranti;* I was bent on finding *comunisti,* and stumbled at last upon a throng of tiny wizened men, clad in suit jackets and tieless shirts meticulously buttoned to the collar, despite the blazing noon heat. Someone assured me these were genuine specimens, true *comunisti,* but the newspaper they were quarreling over was *La Gazzetta dello Sport,* folded to the racing page. The only clue that this might be the

Coniglio arrosto, *roast rabbit, ready to cook at the Trattoria Casa delle Aie in Cervia (recipe page 129).*

Coniglio arrosto *ready to serve at the Trattoria Casa delle Aie in Cervia (recipe page 129).*

ideal workers' state was the free bus ride you got at certain hours, when the automatic punch declined to bite your ticket.

Later, at an *enoteca*—or wine bar, though stocked with an encyclopedic variety of vintages ("la Dotta" again)—I fell into conversation with some students at the university, all *comunisti.* "Do you know what Bologna's symbol is?" asked one, conspicuously *grasso,* gesticulating precisely, as if cradling a baton in his soft fingers. My answer was ready: I even knew how to say "sickle" in Italian. "The symbol," he replied, grinding his plump fist a few inches above his empty wineglass, "is the mortar and pestle." He leaned back in triumph. He explained that these are the tools used to prepare *mortadella,* a shortened form of *mortaio della carne di maiale* ("the mortar of pork meat"), the city's famous sausage, distant kin to our humble baloney. Standards for curing it were formalized in the fourteenth century by Bologna's Guild of Sausage Makers. The first complete recipe for it appears in *Libro novo,* a cookbook published in 1557. (The author recommends soaking the lean pork for three days in *vino rosso,* red wine.) In the film *La Mortadella* (1971), Sophia Loren cannot get past U.S. Customs with her wedding gift, an outsized *mortadella.* Rather than yield it up, she eats it, piece by piece, with help from other travelers.

Bologna is the gateway to Romagna, a region utterly distinct in character from Emilia, though even the editors of the *Enciclopedia italiana* own it is impossible to draw a precise line of demarcation. To the traveler, the differences are unmistakable: Emilia is dominated by the city and the plain, Romagna by the Apennine mountains and the Adriatic coast. Here lie the fourteen mouths of the Po—the most complex delta in Europe, a mazy penetralia of lagoons. The largest lagoon is the Valli di Comacchio, famous for its eel reservoirs. In autumn, the creatures move in a black wriggling mass toward the sea, and farmers scoop them up. Romagnoli cooks grill the catch between bay leaves *(anguilla in gratella)*, soak it in wine vinegar and spices *(anguilla marinata)*, or toss it into thick soups and stews.

The most remarkable city in Emilia-Romagna is Ravenna, on the Adriatic coast. It was for more than three hundred years the leading city in Italy—the seat, first, of Roman emperors (hence *Romagna*) in flight from invaders; then of the invaders themselves, German kings; and finally of Byzantine viceroys, once Ravenna had been recovered by the Emperor Justinian. Amid this tumult, the city burgeoned into the original capital of Western Christian art, thanks to its amazing mosaics, some of them fifteen centuries old—a glitter of spiritualized artistry from an age concededly Dark. Today's pilgrims, tourists, drop coins in a box that bathes the gold tiles in an electric, worldly, and very helpful light.

When my wife and I visited Ravenna some years back, the whole town had turned out to celebrate the *Festa dell'Unità*, the annual communist summer fair, organized that year around a protest of President Reagan's Star Wars. Odd, then, that the featured event was actually a football game, not soccer but American football, rendered convincingly down to the grunts and sideline cheers ("Offense, go!"). The words sounded surreal, but what mortal phrases would not, when uttered on turf where Dante once trod? (He completed the final cantos of the *Paradiso* in Ravenna in 1320, just in time to cross the heavenly threshold—he died, of a fever, in 1321.) And yet, as the afternoon wore on, the spectacle achieved the dignity of an archaic pageant—twenty-two unhorsed paladins clashing with sudden fury, their uniforms soaked with sweat and caked with dirt. It was hard to tell what kept the players going—until some minutes after the game, when they emerged from the locker room. Clad in the crazily inscribed T-shirts that were then the rage ("Dallas-Pittsburgh Yankees"), they were enveloped in the consoling arms of their girlfriends, each as lovely as a fashion model.

Later in the day, after watching the dusky light (no coins needed) coax a blush from the facades of the Piazzale San Francesco, we rose to find our seafood restaurant. There, settling in to a feast of tiny clams and succulent prawns (redolent of lobster), it was possible to believe the *frutti di mare* would always taste this fresh, despite publicized warnings that pollution from offshore oil refineries was already choking the sacred pine groves where Dante once strolled, on the lonely path to paradise.

Sam Tanenhaus

1. *Farmers making hay near Busseto, the birthplace of Giuseppe Verdi, in northern Emilia-Romagna.*

2. *Arcades typical of Modena.*

3. *A farmhouse on an island in the Po di Volano, a region of rivers and canals near Ferrara.*

4. *Fishing nets in fog on the canal near Cervia, on the Adriatic coast south of Ravenna.*

5. *A misty scene near Gussola, between Parma and Mantua.*

6. *Nighttime on the Piazzale San Francesco in Ravenna.*

7. *The castle of Torrechiara, between Langhirano and Parma.*

8. *Le nonne, grandmothers with their sewing and an old friend in front of their house on the road to Imola.*

1

5

2

6

3

7

4

8

Tortelli all'Ortica   Nettle-stuffed Ravioli

From Giancarlo Ceci of the Ristorante Da Ceci, Collecchio

Serves 8

The pasta:

3½ cups all-purpose flour
7 eggs

The filling:

1 pound edible nettles, or raw
    spinach
2 cups ricotta cheese
½ cup grated Parmigiano cheese
¼ pound *mortadella*, finely chopped
    to yield about 1 cup
¼ cup breadcrumbs
1 egg, beaten
½ teaspoon freshly grated nutmeg

1 tablespoon chopped parsley
1 teaspoon peeled and finely
    chopped garlic
2 teaspoons salt
1 teaspoon pepper

The topping:

4 tablespoons (½ stick) butter,
    melted
2 tablespoons chopped fresh sage,
    or ½ tablespoon dried sage
½ cup freshly grated Parmigiano
    cheese

Fresh paste *at the Ristorante Carducci in Modena, top to bottom:* tagliolini, tagliatelle, tortellini, *and* papardelle.

Prepare the dough for the *tortelli* as directed on page 247, using the ingredients listed here.

Wash and trim the nettles or spinach. Boil for 3 or 4 minutes in lightly salted water, drain well, and squeeze dry. When cool, chop fine and mix with the other filling ingredients in a bowl.

Make the *tortelli* with the dough and filling, following the directions for preparation of stuffed pasta on page 247. Make sure they are sealed well around the edges. Cook them in boiling salted water for about 5 minutes, drain, and serve topped with melted butter, sage, and grated cheese.
(Photographs of these tortelli *made with a spinach pasta, pages 124 and 125)*

These tortelli *are a summer specialty of the province of Parma. The filling can be made with spinach, beet greens, or Swiss chard.*

Tortelli alle Erbette   Ravioli with Swiss Chard

From Giancarlo Ceci of the Ristorante Da Ceci, Collecchio

Serves 8

The pasta:

3½ cups all-purpose flour
7 eggs

The filling:

1 pound Swiss chard
1¾ cups ricotta cheese
¼ cup grated Parmigiano cheese
2 eggs
½ teaspoon freshly grated nutmeg

2 teaspoons salt
1 teaspoon pepper

The topping:

4 tablespoons (½ stick) butter,
    melted
2 tablespoons chopped fresh sage,
    or ½ tablespoon dried sage
½ cup freshly grated Parmigiano
    cheese

Follow all of the directions for the *tortelli all'ortica,* above, trimming and boiling the chard instead of the nettles. Serve with the melted butter, sage, and Parmigiano cheese topping.   *(Photograph opposite page)*

◄ OPPOSITE PAGE
Ingredients and the partial preparation for tortelli alle erbette *at the Ristorante Da Ceci in the Villa Maria Luigia (recipe left).*

Making tortelloni all'ortica *with a spinach pasta at the Antica Trattoria del Cacciatore in Bologna (similar recipe made with regular egg pasta, page 123).*

Ragù *sauce in one form or another has traveled the world. Nearly all the regions of Italy have their own variations, using chicken livers, or beef, or pork and veal, or dry white wine instead of red. The amount of tomato used can be adjusted according to personal taste, but it must not be overpowering.*

Ragù is usually made ahead of time, and stored in the refrigerator for a few days, where it improves as the flavors meld. Italians have taken to freezing it in well-sealed containers, since it takes some time to cook, and is very handy to have ready for unexpected guests. Serve ragù bolognese *with* tagliatelle *or another type of pasta, making sure to mix the* ragù *well with the hot pasta in a heated dish so that the pasta is thoroughly impregnated with the sauce. The dish can then be topped with a little butter, and it should be served with plenty of grated Parmigiano cheese to pass at the table.*

Ragù Bolognese   Bolognese Meat Sauce

From Stefano Ferrari of the Antica Trattoria del Cacciatore, Bologna

Serves 6

2 ounces *pancetta*, finely chopped to yield ⅓ cup	3 ounces chicken livers, chopped to yield ½ cup
1 tablespoon butter	1 cup white wine
1 tablespoon olive or vegetable oil	3 tablespoons tomato paste
1 cup peeled and finely chopped onion	1 teaspoon salt
½ cup peeled and finely chopped carrot	1 teaspoon pepper
⅓ cup trimmed and finely chopped celery	½ teaspoon freshly grated nutmeg (optional)
1 pound ground pork, veal, or beef, or a mixture of these	2 cups meat stock, heated
	1 cup cream or milk (optional)

Brown the *pancetta* gently in a large pot with the butter and oil. (Some cooks swear that the *ragù* must be made in an earthenware pot or the flavor is changed dramatically.) Add the chopped onion, carrot, and celery and sauté over medium heat.

When the vegetables have browned, add the ground meat and brown evenly. Add the chopped livers; then in 3 minutes, add the wine and cook until it evaporates. Finally, add the tomato paste and stir. Season with the salt, pepper, and nutmeg if desired, and add the stock. Bring to a boil, cover, lower the heat, and simmer for 2 hours.

Stir the *ragù* occasionally while it is cooking and taste for seasoning, adding salt if necessary. After 2 hours, remove the cover and simmer a while longer to reduce the liquid if the sauce is too runny. Some Bolognese add 1 cup of cream or milk to the sauce at the very end, to make it smoother. *(Photograph opposite page)*

OPPOSITE▶

Traditional paste *served at the Antica Trattoria del Cacciatore: on top,* tortelloni all'ortica *in a butter and sage sauce (similar recipe page 123); on the bottom, a serving of* tagliatelle *topped with* ragù bolognese *(recipe above).*

Freshly cut slices of parmigiano-reggiano *cheese at the Caseificio Rastelli in Rubbiano di Solignano.*

Sformato di carciofi, *artichoke mold, is actually a cross between a British pudding and a soufflé. It takes time to prepare, but uses fewer eggs than a soufflé and is much easier to cook. It can be served alone, or as a side dish (it is recommended as an accompaniment to the veal scallops on page 129). Sformato is difficult to find in restaurants in the region, but figures prominently in home cooking.*

Sformato di Carciofi   Artichoke Mold

From Stefano Ferrari of the Antica Trattoria del Cacciatore, Bologna

Serves 4

6 fresh artichoke hearts, or 2 cups puréed frozen or canned artichoke hearts
Lemon juice
2 tablespoons butter, plus extra to prepare the baking pan

1 cup béchamel sauce (preparation follows)
¼ cup grated Parmigiano cheese
2 eggs, separated
Flour or breadcrumbs to prepare the pan

Preheat the oven to 375°.

If you are using fresh artichokes, remove all their outer leaves by snapping them off above the bottom white part of the leaf. When you have reached the inner "cone," where the leaves are green only at the top 1 inch, cut that top off. Then halve the artichoke vertically, and cut out from each half the small inner leaves and the little hairs (the "beard") beneath them. Pare away some more of the green outer part of the leaves at the base of each half, and cut off the stem. Dribble lemon juice over the prepared artichokes as you complete the others, to keep them from going brown. Cut the artichokes in quarters and boil them for 5 minutes in salted water. Drain well, then sauté them with 2 tablespoons butter in a pan for 5 minutes. Purée the hearts in a food processor or food mill until smooth.

Prepare the béchamel. Mix the artichoke heart purée with the cheese and the béchamel sauce. Beat the egg yolks and add them to the mixture. Whip the egg whites to soft peaks and fold them in. Butter and flour an 8-inch soufflé dish or 4 individual ramekins, and pour the artichoke mixture in. Set the dish in a larger baking dish filled with hot water, and bake for 30 to 40 minutes. The *sformato* should be slightly golden on top.

Leave the *sformato* to cool for about 10 minutes, and then turn it out upside down on a serving dish.

The béchamel:

1½ tablespoons butter
2 tablespoons finely chopped onion
2 tablespoons all-purpose flour
1 cup cold milk

Melt the butter in a small saucepan, add the onion, and sauté over very low heat until the onion is soft. Make sure the butter does not brown.

Whisk in the flour, and cook over low heat, stirring constantly, for about 4 minutes, until the paste is smooth.

Gradually whisk in the cold milk, making sure that the sauce is smooth before adding more milk. When all the milk is whisked in, continue to cook the béchamel over low heat, stirring occasionally, until it thickens. The béchamel will be ready to use in about 5 minutes, but in the traditional Italian preparation it is cooked for as long as 30 minutes.

Men lifting curds into a mold, the first stage in making Parmigiano cheese, at the Caseificio Rastelli in Rubbiano di Solignano.

Alfredo Busani, the quality-control technician of the Caseificio San Giorgio in Soragna, in front of racks of drying Parmigiano cheeses.

An expert testing the quality of the ham at the Quattro Stagioni Prosciuttificio in Langhirano.

Piada bread, familiarly called piadina, is the gastronomic symbol of the rustic Romagna region. It is served hot, wrapped around prosciutto and a soft cheese, and eaten like a sandwich.

Piadina Romagnola Piadina Bread

From Gilberta Santarelli of the Trattoria Casa delle Aie, Cervia

Serves 6

3½ cups flour	2 teaspoons baking powder
6 tablespoons (3 ounces) lard	About 1¼ cups warm water
1 tablespoon salt	

Place the flour on your work surface and make a well in the middle. Add the lard, salt, and baking powder. Add half the warm water and start working the ingredients together, continuing to add water as you blend until you have a firm dough. Knead the dough until very smooth and soft. Form it into small balls and wrap in a floured dishcloth to prevent drying.

Roll out each small ball of dough until quite thin. Heat a griddle to a very, very hot temperature and cook each *piadina* as quickly as possible, piercing the bread with a fork and turning it a few times.

When it is cooked, the *piadina* should be scorched in some places, and almost uncooked in others.   *(Photograph below)*

Women making piadina *bread on an open fire at the Trattoria Casa delle Aie in Cervia (recipe above).*

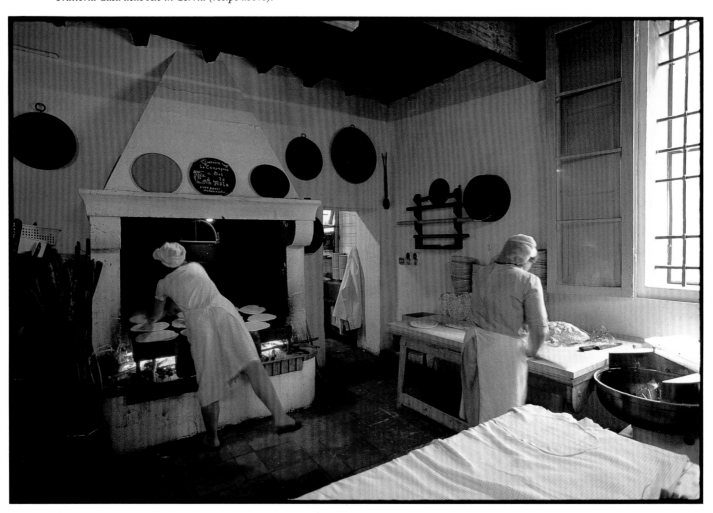

The Trattoria Casa delle Aie in Cervia is on an eighteenth-century farm that was restored, and is now maintained, by the local historical society. It is recognized by the Italian Ministry of Fine Arts as a landmark. Mrs. Gilberta Santarelli is the manager and chief cook.

Baked potatoes are recommended as an accompaniment to this roast rabbit.

Coniglio Arrosto   Roast Rabbit

From Gilberta Santarelli of the Trattoria Casa delle Aie, Cervia

Serves 4

2 teaspoons peeled and finely chopped garlic	½ cup white wine
2 teaspoons chopped fresh rosemary, or ½ teaspoon dried rosemary	½ cup olive oil
	2 young rabbits, cut into joints

One of the glorious mosaics in the chancel of the San Vitale Basilica in Ravenna, depicting the empress Theodora offering the Wine of the Sacrifice.

Mix together the garlic, rosemary, wine, and oil; marinate the rabbit pieces in this mixture in the refrigerator overnight, turning occasionally.

Preheat the oven to 400°.

Place the rabbit pieces in a roasting pan, then pour the marinade over. Roast in the oven for 20 minutes, basting frequently. Turn; then roast 20 minutes longer, basting often.

To serve, place the rabbit pieces on a platter, skim the oil from the juices, and pour the latter over the meat.   *(Photographs pages 118 and 119)*

Sformato di carciofi *(recipe page 126), an artichoke mold, is recommended as an accompaniment to these veal scallops.*

Scaloppine di Vitello   Veal Scallops

From Stefano Ferrari of the Antica Trattoria del Cacciatore, Bologna

Serves 4

Four 4-ounce veal scallops	2 tablespoons butter
1 teaspoon salt	4 thin slices *prosciutto*
½ cup flour	4 paper-thin slices Parmigiano
2 eggs	cheese, or ¼ cup roughly grated
1 cup dried breadcrumbs	¼ cup cream

Preheat the broiler or grill.

Have the butcher flatten the scallops very thin, or do it yourself with a meat tenderizer or the flat side of a cleaver between sheets of wax paper.

Add ½ of the salt to the flour on a plate, and beat the eggs with the rest of the salt in a large shallow bowl. Coat each veal scallop with flour, then dip it into the egg, and then coat with breadcrumbs.

Melt the butter in a large frying pan and cook the veal scallops on each side until golden brown, about 2 minutes a side.

Arrange the veal scallops in a large baking dish. Top each one with a slice of the *prosciutto* and a slice of (or ¼ of the grated) cheese. Pour 1 tablespoon of cream over each, put the dish under the broiler (or a hot grill), and cook until the cheese is golden. Serve with the artichoke mold.

A heated serving tray brimming with the finished result for bollito misto *at the Clinica Gastronomica Arnaldo in Rubiera (recipe right).*

Bollito misto, *mixed boiled meats, is a favorite dish of Emilia-Romagna, but is also found in Piedmont, Lombardy, Tuscany, and in Valle d'Aosta where it is called* lesso, *meaning "boiled." The two different names suggest two distinct preparations, and indeed they are. This recipe from Emilia-Romagna highlights the flavor and succulence of the meats, so the main ingredients are put into the pot when the water is almost boiling, thereby sealing the juices into the meat. In the preparation of* lesso, *all the ingredients are placed in cold water, and in that way the meats give up their best flavors to the broth.*

Serve bollito misto *with* salsa verde, *a piquant green sauce (recipe follows), as they do at the Clinica Gastronomica. Pickles,* mostarda di Cremona, *or vegetables such as carrots, onions, leeks, or potatoes that have been cooked separately are also appropriate on the side. Most Italians prefer nothing but a sauce or a relish to provide a sharp flavor. The broth can be saved and used for other dishes like* cappelletti in brodo *or* risotto. *It can also be kept in the refrigerator for a few days, or frozen.*

Bollito Misto   Mixed Boiled Meats

From Mr. and Mrs. Degoli of the Clinica Gastronomica Arnaldo, Rubiera

Serves 8

2 large carrots, peeled	1 tablespoon each salt and pepper
2 large celery stalks, trimmed	One 2½-pound chicken
2 medium onions, peeled	1 pound veal top round
1 beef tongue (about 2 pounds)	One 1-pound *cotechino* sausage,
1 calf's foot or pig's trotter (about	precooked
1 pound)	One 1-pound *zampone* (stuffed pig's
1 pound beef brisket	trotter sausage), precooked

Put the vegetables, tongue, and calf's foot or pig's trotter into a very large pot with very hot water to cover. Put the pot on high heat, bring to a boil, and skim the froth that forms on the surface. Add the beef brisket and season with salt and pepper. Cover and simmer gently for an hour. Next, add the chicken and veal, and continue to simmer over low heat for another 2 hours. Near the end of this time, add the precooked sausages to the pot, and cook for another 20 minutes.

When you are ready to serve, skin the tongue and slice it very thin. Remove the other meats from the broth. Cut the chicken into the usual parts. Slice the sausages, and carve the remaining meats. Arrange all the meats and chicken on a heated platter, and baste with a little hot broth.
(Photograph above left)

For the *salsa verde:*

4 anchovy fillets packed in oil	¼ cup capers
¼ cup dried breadcrumbs,	½ teaspoon salt
moistened with 2 tablespoons	¼ cup chopped parsley
red wine vinegar	1 cup olive oil
3 cloves garlic, peeled	

Blend all the ingredients but the oil in a blender, then slowly dribble in the oil to make a smooth sauce. Serve with the *bollito misto*.
(Photograph left)

The whole ingredients and blended result for salsa verde *(recipe for a similar sauce, right), a classic accompaniment to* bollito misto.

OPPOSITE ▶
The Enoteca Ca' de Ven, a famous old wine bar and shop in Ravenna.

Looking down on the Roman Forum, a classic view in Rome, with the Coliseum in the background.

A mushroom hunter with his catch in the hills outside of Rome.

Porcini mushrooms from the woods are fried in oil with garlic and salt at the Ristorante La Foresta in Rocca di Papa.

◄ OVERLEAF
The interior of Saint Peter's Basilica in Rome.

VI. *Lazio / Umbria / Le Marche*

WE LOVERS OF ITALY'S DIVERSITY say there is no such thing as an Italian cuisine, but only regional cuisines. After all, until a century ago there was no Italy, only a *minestrone* of perennially warring sovereign provinces. There was no capital, and even today Rome cannot be considered Italy's culinary capital—a title fiercely claimed by the likes of Genoa, Florence, and Bologna.

Our taste buds are happiest in Lazio. No question about it. Here beans are served with chickpeas in a thick broth, a hearty meal in itself. Spaghetti is tastier, with artichokes, broccoli—and clams in their shells in a very light sauce with just a dash of white wine, and just enough red chile peppers to accentuate the subtlety of the clams (an extraordinary combination).

Ever since Marco Polo's homeward voyage, spaghetti has bound the peninsula's disparate regions together, in the same way as the Italian language—loosely. In the watery North people eat the locally grown rice more than pasta, whereas grain thrives in the arid South. Lazio, because of its central location, has access to both these starches, but grain-based pasta is the food of choice.

For pasta is poor people's food, and Roman food is neither aristocratic nor bourgeois, but hearty working-class fare. With the fall of the Caesars, the city lost the tradition of lavish banquets which gave us the adjective "Lucullan," after the extravagant general whose culinary orgies were the talk of the Tiber. The Papacy never developed its own aristocratic cuisine because each new pontiff arrived in the Vatican with his own cooks and provincial recipes. Although the Eternal City never lacked gastronomic glory, Rome was not able to develop its own traditions of fine cuisine, because just as the *monsignore* and the Michelangelos were getting accustomed to Medici spinach or Borgia mutton, His Holiness would pop off and be replaced by a wholly different kettle of fish.

It was in the rural suburbs of Rome, and in the ghetto, that the simple fare which is the glory of today's Lazio developed. Some connoisseurs even insist that Roman food is basically Jewish food. This is because

Lamb and pork on the spit at Gino Ferri's Ristorante La Foresta in Rocca di Papa, a picturesque site south of Rome that is rich in game.

Ingredients for saltimbocca alla romana *in preparation at Da Severino in Rome (recipe page 158).*

the ghetto was the one part of the city unaffected by changes in the Vatican, so Roman-Jewish culinary traditions were the most enduring ones in the city. Interestingly, several of the restaurants in Rome's ancient ghetto are popular with foreign visitors, frequently on the assumption that the food is kosher—which it isn't. If these *ghettorie* are worth visiting, it is for a few Roman-Jewish specialties, notably the *carciofi* (artichokes) *alla giudea* and the deep-fried vegetables. These exquisite artichokes are first cooked whole, then flattened into a flower shape in a simmering frying pan, to come out crisp and mouth-watering.

So what is this Lazio peasant food? *Coda alla vaccinara* (beef tails, in a gravy so thick they almost wag), and *trippa alla romana* (tripe with small tomatoes, garlic, and carrots). And there are so many unusual green vegetables in Lazio, it is truly a vegetarian's paradise. The local *rughetta,* renamed arugula, is everywhere now, including North America. But where is it best? In Lazio, where it is stronger and tarter because they pick it wild. One imagines those little old ladies who sell arugula in the marketplaces rising before dawn and combing the local hillsides to pick it dewy-fresh for their regular customers.

Early summer heralds another wild delicacy: *agretti,* a fleshy, grass-like plant that should be cooked lightly and served with garlic, olive oil, and fresh peppers. Like most produce in the famous Campo dei Fiori, Rome's year-round open market, *agretti* are available for only the few weeks they are in season. That's why over the course of a year you'll find here such a wide variety of vegetables of different sizes and shapes and textures.

Lazio's landscape mirrors the unusual native vegetables. Strange-shaped hills topped with umbrella pines in Druidian circles, precipices sheering off on one side, cork oaks clinging to them: these are the militarily defensible pinnacles where ancient Etruscans and Latins planted their pre-Roman civilizations. The plains are reclaimed marshes, some still-lush wetlands where the mosquito and the water buffalo used to play. Scores of unspoiled medieval towns abound, each sitting atop its own bizarre-shaped mountain, vineyards clinging to the slopes, farmers clinging to the grape arbors, manicuring, picking, grafting, lavishing affection. And the wine grapes are strung up high on arbors for easy access, quite different from their French counterparts; trust the Lazio peasants to make their work pleasant and relaxing.

Temples, aqueducts, and grandiose villas that were the glory of the Roman Empire have left their vestiges everywhere, always choosing the most dramatic sites. In Lazio, you are never more than a few

Ingredients and the finished result for zuppa di castagna, *a simple chestnut soup, at the Ristorante Il Richiastro in the medieval walled town of Viterbo (recipe page 154).*

minutes from an archaeological wonder. Today's average Lazio citizen, including the native-born Roman, has been blessed, not spoiled, by this heritage; he is sophisticated but never pessimistic, self-assured but never truculent, wise but never lacking in humor. He wants to enjoy life himself and he wants you to have a good time too. Food and wine are central pillars of this program.

Radiating out from Rome into the back country of Lazio, we go north and eat fresh trout on the shore of Lake Bracciano, and sip crisp white wine from the nearby fortified towns like Orvieto over the border in Umbria (where an abandoned Carthusian monastery has been converted into a luxury hotel). Cerveteri, southwest of Bracciano, is one of the great "cities of the dead" where the ancient Etruscans were buried in large earthen igloos decorated with frescoes depicting their lives; these tell how important banquets were in that lost civilization. Wines from the local Cerveteri cooperative are full-bodied and nutty-tasting; sold in liter bottles, they are reported to be the purest, least adulterated in Lazio. A few miles away, on a disappointing black lava beach, you can take the sun and swim in a pool at any one of the simple seafood restaurants, and squash down yet more delicious pasta. Today, much of this Mediterranean shore is so polluted that the "local" fish is flown in daily from Casablanca's Atlantic coast. But the Italians remain Europe's savviest connoisseurs of seafood, demanding—and, according to the foreign wholesalers, prepared to pay for—the best and freshest fish available.

What about those glistening caches strewn along the sea wall of Fiumicino's busy little seaport? Were they landed by one of these little fishing boats that bob out into the Mediterranean every day—or did they actually arrive through the adjacent Rome airport? We don't really care to know, because the finest fish restaurants in central Italy are strung out along Fiumicino's main street facing this sea wall, offering seafood spaghetti *in cartoccia,* washed down with open wine from the Alban hills, or a grilled whole sea bass so perfect that the restaurateur chides you for requesting a piece of lemon. These outings in the Roman *campagna* are unforgettable glimpses of light, luscious Lazio.

Vanessa Somers Vreeland

Landlocked between Tuscany (to the north), the Tiber valley (to the east), and the mountainous highlands of Le Marche, Umbria is central Italy's only province without a seacoast. This agricultural area, rich in wooded hills, vineyards, and olive groves, is reminiscent of the Renaissance fresco depicting Umbria's beloved Saint Francis of Assisi talking to the birds. The beauty and mystical serenity found in this masterpiece have survived in Umbria's landscape, which, for the most part, is untainted by the less attractive aspects of the twentieth century. Appropriately, the Italians have christened it "the green heart of Italy." The

A statue on the Campidoglio in Rome, the seat of government in the city since ancient times.

The statue of Pope Paul III inside the Basilica di Santa Maria in Aracoeli, in Rome.

OPPOSITE ▶
Abbacchio arrosto (roast lamb) prepared at the Ristorante Da Severino in Rome.

majority of Umbria's inhabitants are *contadini* (farmers) and artisans who carry on the traditions handed down to them by their Etruscan and Roman forefathers: agriculture, wine making, pottery, carpentry, and most importantly gastronomy, for which they are renowned throughout the peninsula.

Until the turn of the century, the *contadini* ate little meat. Obliged to sell their livestock to ensure a yearly income, they devised the *cucina contadina*, peasant cooking, based on seasonal vegetables and cheese. Food is an important part of Umbria's historic past and social identity which links its folkloric myths and religious rituals. As in Etruscan and Roman times, traditional dishes mark each important occasion from birth to the grave. Never passing up an opportunity for a *festa*, the Umbrians remember their Christian and pagan gods by indiscriminately honoring both throughout the year.

It is therefore inevitable that the kitchen is the hub of the Umbrian farmhouse. Life revolves around the hearth where hot *caffellatte* (coffee with milk), homemade bread, and sheep's cheese see the men off to

A man milking sheep and goats in Castelluccio, in the Sibilline Mountains near Norcia in Umbria.

The interior of the Upper Basilica di San Francesco in Assisi, renowned for its Giotto frescoes. The famous Crucifixion painted by Cimabue in the north transept of the church is in the foreground, to the right.

their fields and the aroma of *sugo* or hot *minestrone* of freshly picked garden vegetables greets them at sunset when the family gather for the evening meal. They are a fun-loving people respected for their earthy honesty and hard work. In fact, a recent study has suggested that the Umbri are the most congenial of all Italians, and that Todi, known for its harmonious atmosphere, is the ideal town in which to live.

I can vouch for that, since I am now restoring an old farmhouse across the valley from Todi. A skilled master builder and his two sons are breathing life back into the thirteenth-century structure. However, at the stroke of noon work comes to a standstill. Their inventive artisanship turns to culinary matters. It is time to roast the sausage and heat the vegetable *frittata* or rabbit stew (prepared by their wives) in a large wrought-iron container kept boiling on a makeshift hearth.

Today, Todi's idyllic tranquility gives no hint of Umbria's violent history. Being of strategic importance on the route from Rome to the Adriatic, Umbria was for centuries a crossroads and battleground. Starting with the Etruscans and followed by the Romans, who in turn were ousted by the Goths and Lombards, bloodshed and pillage were the way of life throughout most of the Middle Ages. Since only six percent of Umbria's territory lies in the plain, her people chose to settle on hilltops. To protect themselves from

Farro all'amatriciana *at the Ristorante La Loggia in the medieval town of Narni in Umbria (recipe page 151). Farro, a hard wheat, is a favorite ingredient of Enzo Scosta, the owner of La Loggia.*

Piatto frescura, *a classic, simple salad of tomatoes, mozzarella cheese, lettuce, and anchovies, at the Ristorante Giardina in the Hotel Umbra in Assisi.*

invasion, they surrounded their towns and villages with fortified walls. The stone houses scramble upward, seemingly clutching each other as if to ensure their safety.

It was in Spoleto that I fell in love with Umbria. For several years I lived and worked in this hill town, and visits to its cathedral awakened my interest in the work of such Renaissance masters as Fra Filippo Lippi, Il Perugino, and Pinturicchio. In Spoleto I had my first taste of Umbrian cooking: *stringozzi* liberally covered with black truffles and a sprinkle of olive oil. *Stringozzi* are known as the *pasta del povero,* the poor man's pasta, as the dough is made from unbleached flour and water and is roughly cut by hand. The contrast between the humble pasta and the fragrant black truffles is unforgettable.

The busiest seasons in Umbria's festive calendar are undoubtedly spring and summer, when produce from the kitchen garden dominates the menu. Ripe tomatoes are made into pulp or dried in the sun in preparation for the winter. Onions, herbs, and garlic are strung into decorative garlands to be hung by the hearth and fruits and berries are simmered down to thick jams ready to spread on the *crostata*—the jam pie eaten on feast days.

In the southeast corner of Umbria sits the town of Norcia, known for its tradition of pig-farming and meat curing. This tradition dates back to the Middle Ages and has made Norcia a household word in Italy. Here every other shop is piled high with tasty, somewhat salty *prosciutto di montagna, pancetta* (bacon), *guanciale alla norcina* (lean bacon from the jowl), *salame,* and *salsicce* (sausages), while wild boar heads hang from the rafters. Patterns of dried *cannellini* beans, lentils, chestnuts, and black truffles fill the display cases. The Norcini take gastronomy seriously. They treat themselves to abundant and lengthy meals which usually include Norcia's most refined and expensive specialty: the black truffle. It is served puréed and spread on toasted bread *(crostini)* or grated on egg *tagliatelle* (recipe page 158), roast pigeon, or the succulent local river trout. In the third week of February truffle lovers and merchants invade the small town to celebrate the *tartufo* festival and to "sniff out" the best buys of Norcia's "black gold."

A more affordable and popular specialty is *porchetta,* the suckling pig fed on chestnuts and acorns which has become a familiar sight at open-air markets and local *feste.* Slices of roast piglet, stuffed with aromatic mountain herbs and garlic accompanied by a slice of country bread, are sold to passersby from roadside stalls. Although relatively few Italians have visited Norcia, the mention of its name conjures up` images of the traditional meal served in every Italian household on New Year's Eve: lentils and *cotechino,* a special pork sausage (recipe page 161). The lentils are said to resemble small coins and symbolize prosperity in the coming year. Another cause for celebration which brings gaiety to the drab winter is the olive harvest. As February comes to a close, the town of Spello is filled with singing olive pickers carrying olive branches. They are joined by the town folk for a feast of hot mulled wine with grilled pork chops and sausages served on a bed of golden polenta (recipe for polenta from the Veneto, page 25).

Umbria produces very good wine but the subject is a bone of contention between the Tuscans and Umbrians. The latter feel that in spite of their restricted production and lesser claim to international fame, the distinct character of the wines grown on the slopes of Orvieto, Torgiano, and Montefalco is more than a match for that of their Tuscan neighbors.

When the building of my house is completed, it will be my turn to give a *festa*—for everyone who has had a hand in the restoration. Decked out in their Sunday best, the workmen and their wives will sit down to a five-course meal followed by dancing. Most likely it will take place in the autumn after the crops are in and the weather has turned cooler. Starting with *salame* and *prosciutto* the menu will continue on with pasta, roast *funghi porcini,* game, and sausage, and will end with the eel-shaped *torciglione* cake decorated with almond fins and flaming cherry eyes, which has been a symbol of fertility and prosperity since Etruscan times.

Nadia Stancioff

◄ OPPOSITE

Dried, cured meats at the Ristorante Dal Francese in Norcia, including prosciutto di cinghiale *(top),* prosciutto crudo *(second from top),* salame, lonza, *and* salsiccia secca *(second row from bottom), and* guanciale *and* pancetta *(bottom row, with more* salame*).*

Prosciutto di agnello e dindo affumicato, *ham of lamb and smoked turkey, served with mushrooms and grated truffles at the Ristorante Dal Francese in Norcia. This dish highlights the* prosciutto *and* tartufi *which are specialties of the town.*

A snowy scene near Urbino, a town most noted for the reign of the colorful Duke Federico da Montefeltro, who made his court here a center for the arts in early Renaissance Italy.

Legend has it that a Roman patrician, upon learning of a friend's banishment by the Emperor, wrote in shock: "To Le Marche? To Le Marche?!" Today this Central Adriatic region remains an enigma even to many Italians, as it is reached through roundabout routes from Rome and Florence or considered a stopover on the road to Abruzzo or farther south. Lack of a superhighway to the capital is cause for rejoicing, at least for the sake of age-old culinary traditions. Le Marche possesses quiet beaches on the Adriatic, hill towns, mountains, and plains, all influencing the unique culinary dishes originating among fishermen, peasants, aristocrats, and shepherds. Farmers living beneath breathtakingly smooth, curving hills prepare *frascarelli*, a flour polenta seasoned not only with the ubiquitous tomato, but sometimes with *mosto cotto*, cooked grape-must, a recipe present in the culinary treatise of the ancient Roman chef Apicius. Behind Urbino, birthplace of the Renaissance master Raphael, lies Novafeltria, a mountainous zone where Umbria, Emilia-Romagna, and Le Marche meet. One characteristic dessert served there is prepared with *tagliatelle*, soft hand-rolled pasta, sprinkled with ground nuts, cinnamon, Alkermes (a red liqueur), and bitter chocolate, a Renaissance tradition yet to be abandoned.

Not far from Urbino is Pesaro, birthplace of Rossini. When he retired from composing operas, Rossini delved into passionate gourmandizing, thereby increasing his girth substantially. "I cried only twice in my life," he mused: "The first time when I heard Paganini play his violin, and the second on a boat when a truffle-stuffed turkey in front of me fell overboard." From Paris he wrote a friend imploring him for Italian olive oil.

Rossini's favorite cellist belonged to the noble Vitali family in Ascoli Piceno, the southernmost city in Le Marche, renowned for its rectangular medieval piazza. Vitali remained a cherished friend, for every year he sent Rossini barrels of the local olives, which provoked the composer to proclaim: "They are the best in all of Europe." The most characteristic dish in Le Marche comes from Vitali's province: *olive farcite* with *crema fritta,* or fried stuffed olives served with rectangles of fried custard. Vitali struck another nerve when his olives were accompanied by truffles, as Le Marche has several locales bearing these prized tubers. Many of Rossini's own recipes demand considerable quantities of truffles as the countryside behind his native Pesaro is rich with *tartufi.* Each autumn the town of Acqualagna celebrates their arrival with a truffle festival.

South of Pesaro is Ancona, famed for its plethora of fish and sea creatures. Outside the town market are stands where ladies expertly shuck oysters and sea truffles. The prize among all are the *balleri,* long, gray, delicately elusive members of the mussel family hiding within craggy rocks. One pope was beside himself with desire for these mollusks, but their extreme fragility could not possibly survive an ordinary journey to Rome. How did the fishermen of Ancona satisfy the papal palate in the days before refrigeration? A new form of sculpture arose from necessity: entire *balleri*-studded rocks were excavated out of the harbor and swathed in cloths drenched with the Adriatic's water, then safely transported across the Apennines to the Vatican's expert chefs. As they are a rare species requiring extreme measures for their capture, commerce today is limited in order to protect the rocky coast along Mount Conero. However, several Ancona restaurants offer this rare delicacy.

The waters off Ancona once abounded with octopuses. Fishermen employing kerosene lamps soon found a purplish mass curiously staring back. When the wooden seventeenth-century Theater of the Muses went up in flames, the glaring light created a scene wildly surpassing the imaginations of the Surrealist painters: tens of thousands of octopuses swarmed to the surface, summoned by the glare. The Anconetani gleefully jumped into their rowboats and scooped them out of the water bare-handed! Along the coast a stew is prepared with octopus, white wine, beet greens, fresh tomatoes, and herbs.

Ancona once had a sizeable Jewish community, which arrived from Portugal in the sixteenth century. One of their prized dishes was goose salami. Their *pan di Spagna,* or Spanish bread, is identical to sponge cake and is still baked throughout Le Marche. During the sixteenth century, Albanian, Slavic, and Armenian traders sailed across the Adriatic from the nearby Ottoman Empire. There remains one culinary trace of those merchants who settled in Le Marche: in Offida, a town *fornaio* bakes and sells *chichí,* pizza stuffed with red and yellow peppers, artichokes, green olives, tuna, and capers, similar to *lahmajiun,* an Armenian dish. The hills around Offida and Ripatransone are gaining a reputation for producing outstanding red wines. Every summer Offida hosts its wine fair inside a medieval cloister.

A farming couple in their field near Roncitelli in Le Marche.

While Napoleon was busy fighting General Windischgrätz near Ancona, the Austrian general had local chefs prepare their lasagne, now known as *vincis-grassi*. Some gastronomes say it is the corruption of a foreign name. A cookbook published ten years before the commander's arrival calls it *princisgrassi*, or "fat for the prince": intended to give stamina to the anemic princes at large. Made with a good dozen layers of thin hand-rolled *tagliatelle* dough, it is stuffed with sweetbreads, or wild mushrooms and meats with a light tomato and béchamel dressing, then baked in a brick oven until the surface is golden and crunchy. What better way to wash it down in country trattorias than with another specialty of the southern Marche: *vino cotto,* or cooked wine. Two liters are boiled down to one, increasing the alcohol content while transforming the flavor into an aromatic Port, as it is brewed with quinces before being decanted into kegs of Rovere oak. The town of Loro Piceno hosts a yearly *sagra* in honor of its special *vino cotto.*

As modern cooking encroaches on ancient traditions, the Marchigiani have kept up ancestral practices to a surprising degree. Their ingenuity works miracles with the humble pig, which once nourished an entire family for the year. Not one part ever goes to waste: salamis and sausages are flavored with five-spice powder and orange rind, then cranked out of tiny cannon-barrel sausage machines. Lard is bottled as a precious cooking fat, *prosciutto* and bacon are set aside, even the skin is cooked and served with boiled potatoes mashed with wild greens gathered from farmhouse gardens. Peasant women took pride in their white hand-embroidered linens, which they washed with homemade soap. Again the pig came to the rescue: all unusable fat scraps were thrown into a caldron with water and caustic soda. Bay leaves were added to create a fragrant aroma. The greatest difficulty faced was one's neighbors: superstition dictated that an envious glance from a neighbor during the soap making was enough to ruin the entire batch. Therefore, the mission was entrusted to the oldest and most experienced women, capable of bringing off their alchemy in undisturbed secrecy.

Travelers to Le Marche will discover more than historic sites such as Urbino, Pesaro, Recanati, Ascoli Piceno, and the Sibilline mountains. A gourmet's journey begins in restaurants serving game, leading on to grocers stocked with local salamis and to innumerable trattorias in villages and along the sea that provide delicacies made with characteristic artisan skill.

Beatrice Muzi

1. *Various dried beans used in the local cooking in Viterbo.*

2. Fritto misto *at the Ristorante Cacciani in Frascati in Lazio includes sweetbreads, lamb's brain, zucchini blossoms, and* porcini *mushrooms.*

3. *A farmer in front of his old house near Pieve Torina, south of Camerino in Le Marche.*

4. Crespelle all'Umbra, *crepes made with ham, cheese, and mushrooms, at the Hotel Umbra in Assisi.*

5. *A woman with her cat and a wheelbarrow full of wild greens for her rabbit, near San Clemente.*

6. Tartufi di mare, *sea truffles, called sea potatoes by some, at the Villa Amalia restaurant in Falconara Marittima.*

7. *A display of fresh fruit in the Campo dei Fiori market in Rome.*

8. *A* zuppa di balleri *from the kitchen of Lamberto Ridolfi and his mother, Amelia, the chef, at the Villa Amalia restaurant in Falconara Marittima.*

9. Pollo alla diavola, *chicken roasted with oil, lemon, and plenty of pepper, at the Ristorante Cacciani in Frascati.*

1

2

3

4

5

6

7

8

9

Zuppa di Cicoria con l'Uovo   Chicory Soup with Egg

From Giovanna Scappucci of the Ristorante Il Richiastro, Viterbo

Serves 4

2 heads chicory, approximately
    2 pounds
½ cup peeled and finely chopped
    onion
3 ounces *pancetta* or bacon,
    chopped to yield ¾ cup
2 teaspoons peeled and finely
    chopped garlic
1½ teaspoons seeded and finely
    chopped serrano chile pepper,
    or ½ teaspoon red pepper flakes

1 tablespoon finely chopped
    fresh mint
¼ cup olive oil
2 cups seeded and chopped fresh
    tomatoes
1 teaspoon salt
4 slices toasted bread
4 eggs

Zuppa di cicoria con l'uovo *at Il Richiastro in Viterbo (recipe left).*

Clean and trim the chicory, and break it into 2-inch pieces.

In a medium-sized pot, sauté the onion, *pancetta*, garlic, chile pepper, and mint in the oil until lightly colored. Add the chopped tomatoes and cook for a couple of minutes. Add the chicory and salt, stir, and cook for another 3 minutes. Add 1 quart of water and simmer for about 30 minutes.

To serve, arrange a slice of toasted bread in each individual serving bowl, break an egg on top, and then pour a couple of ladlefuls of very hot soup over to soak the bread and cook the egg.   *(Photograph right)*

Amatrice is a little mountain town in central Italy. Mr. Scosta confessed that this dish does not have any great history, but was an idea he came up with to indulge his passion for farro, *a hard wheat for which barley is recommended as a substitute.*

Farro all'Amatriciana   Farro Amatrice-style

From Enzo Scosta of the Ristorante La Loggia, Narni

Serves 4

1 cup barley
2 teaspoons salt
3 tablespoons olive oil
2 teaspoons seeded and finely
    chopped serrano chile pepper,
    or ½ teaspoon red pepper flakes
3 ounces *pancetta* or bacon,
    chopped to yield ¾ cup

1 medium onion, peeled and
    thinly sliced
½ cup red wine
One 1-pound can plum tomatoes,
    drained and chopped
½ cup freshly grated Romano cheese

Partially precook the barley: place it in a pot with 3 cups of water and the salt, bring to a boil, cover, and simmer for 45 minutes. Drain before using.

Heat the oil in a medium-sized frying pan and add the chile pepper; then add the *pancetta* and onion and sauté until the onion is limp. Pour in the wine and cook until it evaporates. Add the chopped tomatoes and the drained precooked barley. Simmer gently for about 30 minutes. If necessary, add up to 1 cup of water as the mixture simmers, to prevent the barley from becoming too dry. Serve topped with grated Romano cheese.
(Photograph page 142)

◄ OPPOSITE PAGE
Piccione ripieno, *a roast stuffed pigeon, prepared by chef Cecilioni at the Ristorante Degli Ulivi da Giorgio in Roncitelli.*

In Le Marche and on the Adriatic coast, fish soup is known as brodetto. *Fish is notably good on this coastline, and several towns have their own versions of* brodetto; *those of Rimini, Ravenna Marina, and Ancona are well known.*

Here is the recipe for fish soup as it is made near Ancona. It is up to the resourcefulness and imagination of the cook to devise something as good with available fresh fish. The fish used for the brodetto *should be of two or three different varieties. Serve the soup hot with slices of toasted bread (*bruschetta, *recipe page 208).*

Brodetto   Fish Soup

From the Hotel Emilia, Portonovo di Ancona

Serves 4

1 pound assorted fish fillets (cod, sole, red snapper, and the like)	3 tablespoons olive oil
	1 teaspoon salt
1 pound squid, cleaned, bone and ink discarded	½ teaspoon pepper
	½ teaspoon powdered saffron, dissolved in 1 tablespoon water
½ cup peeled and finely chopped onion	1 cup dry white wine

Cut the fish fillets into 2-inch strips. Cut the squid into ¼-inch rings.

Sauté the chopped onion in the olive oil, then add the squid, season with salt and pepper, and add the saffron. Cook for about ¾ of an hour over low heat. Then add the rest of the fish in layers, with the most delicate kinds at the top, and pour in the wine. Cook until the wine is reduced by half, then add 2 cups water. Simmer gently for about 10 minutes, then taste and correct the seasoning to serve.   *(Photographs above right and opposite page)*

Brodetto *ready to serve at the Hotel Emilia in Portonovo di Ancona (recipe for a similar* brodetto, *left).*

◄ OPPOSITE PAGE
Ingredients for a brodetto *at the Hotel Emilia in Portonovo di Ancona (recipe for a similar* brodetto, *left).*

Bucatini all'Amatriciana   Bucatini Pasta Amatrice-style

From the Cacciani family of the Ristorante Cacciani, Frascati

Serves 4

1 cup peeled and finely chopped onion	1 teaspoon seeded and finely chopped serrano chile pepper, or ¼ teaspoon red pepper flakes
3 tablespoons olive oil	
6 ounces *pancetta* or bacon, chopped to yield 1½ cups	Salt to taste
1 teaspoon peeled and finely chopped garlic	1 pound *bucatini* or *perciatelli* pasta
½ cup white wine	⅔ cup grated Romano cheese, plus extra for topping
One 28-ounce can plum tomatoes, finely chopped, with liquid	1 tablespoon rinsed and chopped fresh basil leaves (optional)

Sauté the chopped onion in the oil in a large pan until golden brown. Add the *pancetta* and the garlic and continue cooking for about 5 minutes. Pour in the wine and cook until it evaporates, then add the tomatoes and their liquid, chile pepper, and salt. Simmer for about 30 minutes.

Cook the pasta in plenty of boiling salted water until *al dente*. Drain and toss with the sauce, cheese, and basil if desired, in a serving dish. Serve with more grated cheese on the side.   *(Photograph right)*

Ingredients for bucatini all'amatriciana *at the Ristorante Cacciani in Frascati (recipe left).*

Zuppa di cozze e zucchini, *cooked and ready to serve at the Villa Amalia (recipe right).*

Zuppa di Cozze e Zucchini   Mussel and Zucchini Soup

From Amelia Ceccarelli of the Villa Amalia, Falconara Marittima

Serves 6

4 pounds mussels in their shells	¾ cup dry white wine
1 medium onion, peeled and thinly sliced	1¼ cups seeded and chopped fresh ripe tomatoes, or a 1-pound can plum tomatoes, drained and chopped
½ cup extra virgin olive oil	
1 teaspoon peeled and finely chopped garlic	
1 teaspoon seeded and finely chopped serrano chile pepper, or ¼ teaspoon red pepper flakes	Pinch of sugar (optional)
	2¼ cups washed, trimmed, and cubed zucchini
1 tablespoon chopped capers	1 tablespoon rinsed and chopped fresh basil leaves
1 red sweet pepper, washed, seeded, deveined, and cut into strips	¼ teaspoon grated lemon peel
1 yellow sweet pepper, washed, seeded, deveined, and cut into strips	1 teaspoon salt
	½ cup milk
	2 tablespoons finely chopped parsley

Wash and clean the mussels thoroughly.

In a large pan, cook the onion in the oil until limp, then add the garlic, chile pepper, capers, and sweet peppers. Cook for 5 minutes. Pour in the wine and simmer until it evaporates; then add the tomatoes and the sugar if desired, and cook for another 10 minutes.

In a separate pot, toss the zucchini into boiling salted water and stir; as soon as the water comes to the boil again, drain. Add the zucchini, basil, and lemon peel to the other ingredients, continue cooking for a few minutes, and season with salt. Finally, add the milk and mussels, cover, and cook for 10 minutes more. (Some people prefer to cook the mussels separately. To do so, place the mussels in a pot over high heat and cover. Cook for a few minutes, until the shells open. Drain the mussels and add to the vegetables.) Remove most of the mussels from their shells to make them easier to eat, leaving just a few in their shells for decoration. Sprinkle with parsley, and serve. *(Photographs above left and opposite page)*

Zuppa di Castagna   Chestnut Soup

From Giovanna Scappucci of the Ristorante Il Richiastro, Viterbo

Serves 4

2 cups dried chestnuts	chopped serrano chile pepper, or ¼ teaspoon red pepper flakes
2 teaspoons peeled and chopped garlic	2 tablespoons olive oil
1 teaspoon seeded and finely	1 teaspoon salt

Soak the dried chestnuts in water overnight. Drain and rinse them the next day, removing any leftover skin. Put the chestnuts in a pot, cover with 2 quarts of water, and simmer over low heat for 1 hour.

Make a *soffritto* base by sautéing the chopped garlic and pepper in the oil in a frying pan for a minute or 2. Pour the *soffritto* into the pot with the chestnuts to flavor; continue cooking for a few minutes. Use a wire whisk to break up the chestnut pieces. Allow to cook for a few minutes longer, then season with the salt, and serve.   *(Photograph page 137)*

OPPOSITE PAGE ▶
Ingredients for zuppa di cozze e zucchini *at the Villa Amalia restaurant in Falconara Marittima, Ancona (recipe above right).*

Stringozzi all'Oliva   Pasta with Black Olive Sauce

From Mr. and Mrs. Laudenzi of the Ristorante Giardina, Assisi

Serves 4

The pasta:

2 cups all-purpose flour
1 egg white
½ cup water
Pinch of salt
2 tablespoons olive oil

The sauce:

1 pound fresh *champignon* mushrooms, or button mushrooms
1 teaspoon peeled and finely
   chopped garlic

3 tablespoons olive oil
2 cups pitted black olives
¼ cup chopped parsley
4 tablespoons (½ stick) butter
1 teaspoon seeded and finely
   chopped serrano chile pepper,
   or ¼ teaspoon red pepper flakes
Salt to taste
½ cup cream

½ cup freshly grated Parmigiano
   cheese

The traditional preparation of stringozzi
*pasta at Mr. and Mrs. Laudenzi's
Ristorante Giardina in the Hotel Umbra
in Assisi.*

Prepare the pasta dough with the ingredients listed here following the directions on page 247. Work the dough well until it becomes nice and firm; when
ready, roll it out twice as thick as usual (the 4th from last thickness on a
machine), and cut it like *tagliatelle*. One pound of purchased *cavatelli* or
tagliatelle can also be used.

To make the sauce, clean and rinse the mushrooms thoroughly, and cut
them into thick slices. Sauté the garlic in a frying pan with the olive oil. Add
the mushrooms and stir. Sauté for about 5 minutes, then blend the sautéed
mushrooms with the olives and parsley in a food processor.

Cook the pasta in plenty of boiling salted water until *al dente* (just a
minute or 2 if you have made it fresh). Melt the butter in a large frying pan,
add the olive/mushroom mixture, cook for about 5 minutes with the chile
pepper, and salt to taste. Stir in the cream at the end.

Drain the *stringozzi* and toss with the sauce and Parmigiano cheese to
serve.   *(Photographs above right and opposite page)*

Strings of onions and garlic at the market in Spoleto in Umbria.

◄ OPPOSITE
   Ingredients for stringozzi all'oliva *ready
   to be assembled at the Ristorante
   Giardina in Assisi (recipe above).*

A serving of tagliatelle con funghi e tartufo *at Dal Francese in Norcia (recipe right).*

Truffles in Umbria are black and come from the Valle Valnerina near Norcia and Spoleto. Scheggino is the main market center for this highly prized produce. Hunted out from October to March by specially trained dogs, black truffles are not quite as powerful in taste or scent as the white truffles of Piedmont.

Vittorio Battilocchi, proprietor of a charming restaurant in Norcia, preserves black truffles in cans and vacuum packs them in such a way that they retain virtually all of their flavor. He uses truffle shavings on everything—pastas, eggs, meats—almost like parsley. He has even gone so far as to make his own gelato al tartufo *with the help of a local ice-cream parlor.*

Tagliatelle con Funghi e Tartufo

Pasta with Mushroom Sauce and Truffle

From Vittorio Battilocchi of the Trattoria Dal Francese, Norcia

Serves 4

4 tablespoons (½ stick) butter	1 pound *tagliatelle,* fresh or dried
1 pound fresh *champignon* mushrooms, or button mushrooms, stemmed, washed, and sliced not too thin	½ cup freshly grated Parmigiano cheese
	Milk (optional)
	Black truffle

Melt the butter in a large pan and sauté the mushrooms over medium heat until they are cooked through, and most of their juice has evaporated.

Cook the *tagliatelle* in plenty of boiling salted water until it is *al dente* (for directions to make fresh *tagliatelle,* see page 247). Drain and transfer the pasta to the pan with the mushrooms. Add the cheese and toss well. Add a little milk if you want more sauce—do not add more butter, as it makes the dish too rich. Serve with the truffle grated on top.   *(Photograph above left)*

Saltimbocca alla romana *ready to eat at Da Severino in Rome (recipe right).*

This very quick dish is so common in the city that it is virtually synonymous with Rome. The name, saltimbocca alla romana, *literally means "jump into the mouth, Roman-style." Though dried sage can be substituted here, fresh is strongly recommended.*

Saltimbocca alla Romana   Veal Slices with Prosciutto

From Mr. and Mrs. Severino Severini of Da Severino, Rome

Serves 4

Eight 3- to 4-ounce veal scallops	½ cup flour
¼ pound *prosciutto* cut into 8 slices, with the rind removed	6 tablespoons (¾ stick) butter
8 fresh sage leaves, or 1 teaspoon dried sage	Salt and pepper to taste
	1 cup dry white wine (optional)

Pound the veal slices gently to make them an even thickness. Lay a slice of *prosciutto* and a sage leaf on each, then pin the *prosciutto* and sage to the veal slice with a toothpick inserted through the meat. (If you are using dried sage, ⅛ teaspoon should be sprinkled on each veal slice, *after cooking.*) You can also roll each slice up with the *prosciutto* and sage inside, and fix with a toothpick. Dust each slice lightly with flour.

In a large frying pan, cook the veal gently over medium heat in 4 tablespoons of the butter until well browned all over (approximately 2 minutes per side). Add salt and pepper. If desired, pour the wine into the pan and turn up the heat, allowing the wine to evaporate quickly.

Remove the veal from the pan and place on a warm serving platter. Put the remaining 2 tablespoons of butter into the pan over low heat, and stir and scrape the bottom and edges of the pan to pick up any loose bits. Pour this over the *saltimbocca* and serve.
(Photographs opposite page, bottom, and page 136)

Serve this veal stew with vegetables such as chicory sautéed with garlic and rosemary, sweet-and-sour onions, or trifolati *mushrooms, sautéed with garlic and parsley (recipe page 28).*

Pasticciata alla Pesarese   Roast Veal, Pesaro-style

From Maurizio Cecilioni of the Ristorante Degli Ulivi da Giorgio, Roncitelli

Serves 6

Pasticciata alla pesarese *at the Ristorante Degli Ulivi da Giorgio in Roncitelli (recipe left).*

2 pounds veal top round
¼ cup flour
¼ cup olive oil
1½ cups peeled and chopped onion
¾ cup peeled and chopped carrot
⅔ cup trimmed and chopped celery
2 teaspoons peeled and finely
   chopped garlic
Aromatics: ¼ teaspoon fennel seed,
   2 sage leaves (or ¼ teaspoon dried
   sage), 1 sprig rosemary (or ¼ teaspoon dried rosemary), 1 bay leaf

1 tablespoon salt
2 teaspoons pepper
1 bottle (3½ cups) dry white wine
6 cups meat stock
½ tablespoon tomato paste
½ cup chopped canned plum
   tomatoes with their juice

Pat the meat dry and dust it with the flour. Quickly brown the meat on all sides with 2 tablespoons of the olive oil in a hot skillet to seal in the juices.

In a very large pot, sauté the onion, carrot, and celery with the chopped garlic and aromatics in the remaining 2 tablespoons of the oil until golden. Add the meat, season with 2 teaspoons of salt and 1 teaspoon of pepper, pour in the wine, and simmer over medium heat until it reduces to about ½ cup of liquid. Add the stock and partially cover the pot.

Simmer for 2½ hours over medium heat, turning the meat every ½ hour. Add more stock if needed.

When the meat is tender when pricked with a fork, remove it, the stems of the aromatics, and the bay leaf from the pot, and blend all the vegetables and liquid in a food processor or blender to make a thick sauce. Return the sauce to the pot and add the tomato paste, chopped tomatoes, ½ teaspoon salt, and ¼ teaspoon pepper, and cook for about 15 minutes longer. The sauce should have a fairly thick consistency; you may want to adjust the seasoning once more. Slice the veal and reheat the slices in the sauce to serve.
(Photograph above right)

Lentils from the small mountain village of Castelluccio are considered the best in Italy. They are tiny, brown, and extremely delicate. When they are in flower, the valley where they grow has a pale blue, misty atmosphere. The sausages in this recipe are a specialty of Norcia, but any kind can be used, depending on the preference of the cook.

Salsicce con Lenticchie   Sausages with Lentils

From Vittorio Battilocchi of the Trattoria Dal Francese, Norcia

Serves 4

1½ cups brown lentils
2 ounces *pancetta*, finely chopped
   to yield ⅓ cup
2 tablespoons olive oil
⅓ cup peeled and finely
   chopped onion
1 cup trimmed and finely
   chopped celery

2 teaspoons peeled and finely
   chopped garlic
2 pounds Italian sausage links
2 teaspoons salt
1 teaspoon pepper

Ingredients for salsicce con lenticchie *waiting to be prepared at Dal Francese in Norcia (recipe left).*

Cover the lentils with water and soak them in a bowl for 1 hour.

In a large pan, sauté the *pancetta* in the olive oil over low heat for 5 minutes. Add the onion and celery, and cook until the vegetables are soft. Add the garlic and cook for 2 minutes. Drain the lentils, add them to the pan, and sauté them for a minute. Then cover them with 3 cups of fresh water. Simmer for about 20 minutes, adding a little water if the lentils get too dry.

While the lentils are cooking, fry the sausages whole in another pan until they are thoroughly cooked.

About 5 minutes before the lentils are done, season them with the salt and pepper. Serve the sausages with the lentils as a side dish.

(Photographs right and opposite page)

A shepherd with his flock coming down the valley to the milking station near Castelluccio in the Sibilline Mountains.

◄ OPPOSITE
Vittorio Battilocchi's salsicce con lenticchie, *cooked and ready to be eaten at Dal Francese in Norcia (recipe above).*

In Norcia, Umbria, cherries and sugar are put into a jar and left in the sun to melt together.

Brustengolo   Corn Flour Cake

From Mr. and Mrs. Laudenzi of the Ristorante Giardina, Assisi

Serves 6

3½ cups peeled, cored, and sliced
  Granny Smith apples
2 tablespoons fresh lemon juice
2 cups sugar
⅞ pound (3½ sticks) butter, melted,
  plus extra to prepare the pan
3¼ cups corn flour, plus extra
  to prepare the pan
1½ teaspoons baking powder

4 eggs
⅓ cup coarsely chopped pine nuts,
  toasted in the oven
⅓ cup coarsely chopped walnuts
2 tablespoons golden raisins,
  coarsely chopped and soaked
  in 2 tablespoons anisette
  or Pernod liqueur
1 teaspoon grated lemon peel

Preheat the oven to 350°.

Place the apple slices in a bowl and sprinkle them with the lemon juice.

Mix the sugar and melted butter in a large bowl with a wooden spoon, then fold in the flour and baking powder. Beat in the eggs until the mixture is smooth, then add the pine nuts, walnuts, raisins, liqueur, and grated lemon peel. Finally, add the drained sliced apples to the dough, and stir thoroughly.

Butter and flour a 9-inch springform pan, pour in the cake batter, and bake in the oven for about an hour.

When the cake is done, remove it from the oven and allow it to cool to room temperature in the pan before serving.   *(Photograph opposite page)*

A hilly landscape near Sassoferrato, northwest of Fabriano in Le Marche.

OPPOSITE▶

A selection of local cakes at the Ristorante Giardina in the Hotel Umbra in Assisi, top to bottom: grigliata Umbra, *made with dried fruit;* brustengolo, *made with apples (similar recipe above); and* grigliata di ricotta, *made with ricotta cheese.*

VII. *Abruzzi / Campania / Calabria*

I ONCE CONTRIVED TO HAVE A MAN fall in love with me by telling him I had grown up eating flowers and blood—squash flowers and blood sausage. I knew the juxtaposition would please him: there is lyricism in Italian food, and particularly in the food of the South, earthy and romantic, delicate and strong (lamb's head and rosemary, pork liver and bay leaf, truffles and beans).

Federico Secondo (Frederick II)—falconer, astronomer, Crusader, heretic—ruled what is now Abruzzo/Molise in the thirteenth century. The poetry of Southern Italian food is as real as that which resides in his castles and in Roman ruins; it is the poetry of the Adriatic, and the Mediterranean, and of the wild and welcoming Apennine mountains.

In folk tales from the Abruzzo—the province of Italy east of Rome that extends to the south of it, a part of the Mezzogiorno in equal measure beautiful and harsh—food is used as the language of love: a king's son, slicing fresh ricotta, spills a drop of blood on that whiteness, and "Mama," he says (in a story recounted by Italo Calvino), "I would like a wife white like milk and red like blood. . . . Milk-white and blood-red." And, obligingly, a beautiful milky maiden jumps out of a pomegranate.

The Jordan River, we are told in another story, has a weakness for ring-shaped cakes, "which he enjoyed twirling in his whirlpools." My grandmother made those ring-shaped cakes in her kitchen (the center and heart of family life); they were called *tiralles*; hard and plain, they are valued for their cunning shape: they look like the coiled serpents Abruzzo's ancient Marsi peoples worshipped. Grandmother made *ferratelle*, too—thin, patterned cookies cooked in a kind of waffle iron (with a different pattern on each side), and, for Christmas, a pyramidical sweet called *cicerchiata*, hollow balls held together with honey and sprinkled with tiny colored-sugar beads.

Cakes are made of mountain ricotta, a cheese so rich it is often served, dusted with chocolate or covered with crushed mulberries, blueberries, or ripe raspberries, as a dessert. The mozzarella of Abruzzo, a

◄ OPPOSITE
The ingredients and process of making maccheroni alla chitarra, *at the Hotel Villa Santa Maria in the town of that name. This is the traditional way of making pasta in the Abruzzi. The dough is placed over the pasta cutter (which can be "tuned" like a guitar* (chitarra) *for different widths of pasta) and then pressed down with a rolling pin.*

◄ OVERLEAF
The medieval village of Pacentro in the hills above Sulmona, birthplace of the Latin poet Ovid.

A column capital detail from the twelfth-century church of San Leonardo, located near the town of Manfredonia on the Gargano Massif, a huge limestone plateau that juts out right above the "heel" of Italy, south of Molise in Apulia.

cheese without equal, is made from the milk of buffalo who graze on aromatic mountain grasses, clover, thyme . . . as do the lucky sheep from which *pecorino* cheese comes, and the cows from which *scamorza*, a cheese often served *in carrozza*—fried between slices of wheat bread—comes. Each local dairy has its own variation on the classical cheeses of Abruzzo . . . which is a country of contrasts: it is not surprising—though it is delicious to contemplate—that Abruzzesi take equal delight in sausages and sweets.

"A woman is always buying something," Ovid, the poet of Sulmona, wrote; and in Sulmona the thing to buy is *torrone* (honey-almond or chocolate-hazelnut nougat), and *confetti*. . . . Dickens was mad for *confetti*, which rained, in Rome, from balconies at Carnevale. . . . The candy stores of Sulmona are enchanted gardens: *confetti* in the shape of Victorian nosegays; cherries red as love-bitten lips; sheaves of wheat; sunflowers; cat-o'-nine-tails; bunches of yellow, blue, orange, purple, pink grapes, all made from sugared almonds wired together and covered with colored cellophane. . . .

And one goes from contemplating this sugary beauty to the dining table, where one eats robust *pasta e fagioli*, macaroni and chickpeas in bean-thickened sauce, a transition from poetry to prose. . . .

L'Aquila, the capital of Abruzzo, is situated nicely in a basin of land surrounded by the purple-blue mountains of the Gran Sasso, the tallest peaks of the Apennines. Every morning, in the pale gold light of dawn, silver trucks pull into the generous Piazza del'Duomo; in them are great wood-burning ovens, on which are roasted, on huge spits, whole suckling pigs redolent of rosemary—portable feasts. Strings of liver sausage, sweetened with honey or spiced with chile peppers, alternate with *mortadella* sausages—lean pork meat, with a core of fat—which are sold in pairs.

Italians believe that the liver is the part of the human body most susceptible to bodily ills; and perhaps for this reason they have great faith in the efficacy of animal livers, regarding pork liver as the medical specific for rheumatism, lumbago, puberty, and crankiness. Crescent-shaped and wrapped in a caul of white membrane, it is surprisingly delicate.

The happy manager of an inn in Ladispoli, outside Rome, believes that the best chefs in Italy come from Chieti, in Abruzzo. He remembers the sweet-and-spicy smell of the closets of Abruzzo—where bladder sausages, parboiled and stuffed with apples, are hung to dry.

Chieti is on the sea, from which comes a humble but ravishing cuisine: peppery squid *in purgatorio*; grilled mullet; a kind of sea frog that fishermen stew; whitefish soup; *scungilli*, a large snail, the bland, rubbery meat of which miraculously transforms tomato sauce into a gravy of incredible richness; and *baccalà*—salted codfish which stands like planks along shop fronts and is soaked in many waters before it contributes its strong flavor to tomato sauce.

A lovely old woman's face, "as rugged as the region," near Pietraferrazzana in Molise.

OPPOSITE▶

Peperoni in padella at the Santa Maria Ristorante in Villa Santa Maria, near Chieti in the Abruzzi. To prepare, simply wash and clean red peppers, cut them in strips, and sauté in olive oil in a covered pan over medium heat for about twenty minutes, stirring occasionally.

A Sunday family lunch al fresco, *outdoors, but in the shade, near Mignano Monte Lungo in Campania.*

A group of family and friends outside a bar in Lentiscosa, near the Gulf of Policastro in Campania.

The blessing of the sea mists is one of the reasons for the delectability of Italian vegetables—escarole, and broccoli rape, and red and yellow peppers (which, roasted and served with garlic and oil or mixed with fried eggs or stewed with veal, are sweeter in Southern Italy than they are any place else in the world). The sweetness of the mountain grasses is the reason given for the succulence of animal flesh.

Abruzzesi don't need reasons. It is enough for them to celebrate the abundant evidence. Any town that has a gastronomic or agronomic specialty (and that is practically every town) has a festival—a strawberry festival; a lamb festival; a festival of lentils and sausages. There is a festival of broad beans, which are often served with marjoram and sometimes with mint, which is believed by the pious to be Mary's herb, one she needed for her poor stomach when Jesus died. There is a chestnut festival: Abruzzo makes *pizza con le foglie*, a cornmeal pie baked in a hot oven under chestnut leaves, over which a broth of pigs' feet, ears, and snouts, potatoes, tomatoes, and garlic is poured together with boiled greens. There are festivals of pine nuts, trout, crayfish, chickens, *castrato*—tender mutton—and pig. . . . The skin, or rind, of the pig is

Alici marinate, *fresh anchovies marinated in vinegar and salt, then served with a sauce of lemon, oil, vinegar, hot peppers, parsley, onion, oregano, and garlic by Alfonso at his restaurant in Praiano on the Amalfi coast. This preparation differs from the usual anchovies in oil or brine. The anchovies are very delicate and difficult to find as, like fresh sardines, they are caught only during the waning moon.*

stuffed with pine nuts, raisins, parsley, and garlic and placed in tomato sauce for pasta. . . . There is a festival of truffles.

White and black truffles are common in the southern Apennines, and so are *porcini*, meaty wild boletus mushrooms. There is no happier time in Italy than the season when truffles and *porcini* coincide. With the addition of onions and *pecorino* they gorgeously flavor *risotto*. (Abruzzo grows saffron, too.)

Rice is indigenous to Abruzzo; but pasta from durum wheat, dry and fresh, is the food most closely associated with the South. Abruzzo is famous for its *spaghetti alla chitarra*, made on a wood-and-wire instrument that resembles a guitar (and that, like a guitar, can be "tuned" to produce different sizes and textures of pasta). It is particularly good served with shredded lamb in garlic sauce. I had this dish in Molise, the district south of Abruzzo, which was made a separate administrative entity in 1963, but which is, as to food and culture and geography, hardly distinguishable from Abruzzo; the *spaghetti* was preceded by marinated anchovies and shellfish and cold *calamari*, and followed by asparagus and spinach in lemon and olive oil.

"Olives nourish me," Horace said. I think of this when I am in Molise, in Venafro, my grandmother's town, which Horace loved. The oil of the first pressing, a lapidary pale green, is practically a food in itself.

There is in Abruzzo and Molise a feast called *panarda* "that starts again," food historian Gian Gaspare Napolitano said, "when it finally seems over . . . an avalanche of food." Held for any or no reason at all, "it has survived famines, the ravages of invasion and war."

What doesn't kill you fattens you, Italians say.

Once, in the town of Avezzano, I attended a six-hour First Communion feast; my food-drugged memory allows me to recall melon (sculpted to resemble flowers) and *prosciutto; stracciatelle* in turkey broth; lasagne with béchamel and meat sauce; spaghetti with shellfish; fish fry; quail with rosemary-roasted potatoes; chicory salad; spinach in olive oil; ices; fruit and cheese; *gelato*; a dense chocolate fruitcake with white sugar frosting; open-face sandwiches made with butter, walnuts, and truffles; cream puffs tinted pink and green and pale yellow to look like peaches and filled with peach liqueur, with chocolate "pits" and candied green stems. When I expressed incredulity, I was told by my host: *"Credete e amate, mangia in pace"*: Believe it and love, eat in peace.

Molise has been called the "hillbilly country" of Italy. In the little Molisano town of Pietrabbondante,

Alfonso preserves his own capperi, *capers, with their leaves, picked fresh from the hills above his house, by storing them weighted in coarse salt for at least twenty days, then washing them, soaking them with vinegar, and keeping them in jars with olive oil. He serves the* capperi *and their leaves, marinated with garlic and hot dried peppers, as an antipasto, accompanied by tomatoes and bread.*

I saw a play by Genet performed in an ancient Roman amphitheater, and had *tagliatelle* with *porcini*—hardly a hillbilly dish. In Isernia, the capital of Molise, I had *risotto* with a tomato-based fish sauce; and kids' heads baked in terracotta bowls with oil, dry white wine, parsley, ewes' milk, cheese, egg yolk. Cornmeal mush (polenta) mixed with red beans flavored with *pecorino*, onions, and paprika is country fare, but it is so simple it is exquisite. So is *cavatelli* with broccoli rape. Broccoli rape looks like a cross between turnip greens and broccoli, but tastes like neither; it has a slightly and pleasantly bitter, astringent taste that goes well with the "fatness" of the noodles, into which one's teeth almost obscenely sink. Grilled small cuttlefish, minced squid, sand crabs, prawns, clams, mussels, cooked in tomato sauce with peppers and cloves and basil and olive oil. Partridges; stuffed pigeons; wild boar. And all this washed down with good white wine—Trebbiano; and noble red wine, Montepulciano of Abruzzo.

The first time I went to Abruzzo/Molise I came home with one regret: that I hadn't brought with me the liqueurs, *digestivi* and *amaros*, pre- and post-dinner drinks, common to that region, and unavailable outside of it, the most famous of which is Centerbe—a hundred herbs—pale green fire. I like the Doppio Arancia (double-orange) liqueur of Abruzzo, and Maiella (honey) *amaro*. Best of all I like the sweet syrupy brown liqueur made in the little town of Cocullo, where, every year, on the first Thursday of May, the men and boys of the village go up into the hills and search for snakes, which they offer, with expectation of impunity, to useful St. Dominick, who protects the Abruzzesi from snakebite, rabies, and toothache. I like this *amaro*—it tastes like alcoholic Coca-Cola—because it has a picture of snakes twined around a church on its label.

The wine with the most beautiful name is Lacrima Christi, which comes from Campania, the crescent of land around the Bay of Naples, a land of unambiguous, kaleidoscopic light, terraced vineyards, lemons and oranges and pastel houses and death-defying roads that wind and climb higher and higher into a world of flowers and sun—the beauty increases as the danger does, and the danger, so great is the beauty, seems not to matter. Almond blossoms and the sirens of Capri, volcanoes, and the ravishing Mediterranean Sea, as spectacularly beautiful as Naples is spectacularly degraded, decaying, corrupt, sad. Lacrima Christi means "tears of Christ." Everything lovely, and everything sad.

The Neapolitans invented pizza. They invented pasta, too. Macaroni is mentioned in Boccaccio's *Decameron*. No Italian alive believes that Marco Polo brought macaroni back from China to Italy. The white clam sauce of Naples and the red clam sauce of Naples, made with tomatoes, are justly famous. The tomato, without which it is impossible to imagine Italian cuisine, came to Italy from Spain, by way of America. It is odd to think that macaroni predates tomato sauce—there are old engravings of Neapolitans walking around eating sticks of gummy pasta, a kind of finger food.

◄ OPPOSITE
An assortment of antipasti *made with goat cheese and fresh local vegetables marinated in various combinations of olive oil, vinegar, lemon juice, garlic, onions, and fresh herbs, served at the Ristorante Cappuccini Convento in Amalfi.*

A pregnant woman with a squash on her head in the Abruzzi.

I have had some of the most memorable meals of my life in Campania: in Sorrento, under an umbrella of orange blossoms overlooking the sea (which is reached by Etruscan stairs carved in tunneled cliffs), veal chops grilled with basil and butter; in the cozy little town of Sant'Agnello, *arancini*—breaded and fried rice balls stuffed with spicy chopped meat and raisins and pine nuts held together with tomato sauce (recipe for *arancini* from Sicily, page 244); and fish fries with baby anchovies and *calamari* and *scampi*. And new zucchini fried in olive oil with drops of vinegar to sweeten it—I had this zucchini with country bread and fried sweet *provolone* and thin slices of *prosciutto*, and greengage plums, in the house of a friend set in the middle of a walled garden on a terrace above which a little train—the Circumvesuviana—chugged its way between Sorrento and Naples, like a train in a child's dream, a garden of flowering lemon trees.

Yellow squash flowers dipped in a batter of flour and egg, and fried.

In a restaurant where Wagner ate, evil-looking lobsters are displayed next to baroque meringues.

I drink *orzata*—the milk of crushed almonds which looks like the milk of pearls—in the public gardens of Capri, the *faraglioni*, those thrusting, sheltering rocks that seem as much a part of the unconscious as of the sea, insistently reminding us of paradise found . . . lost . . . found. . . .

Penne arrabbiata (*arrabbiata* means angry) in Amalfi, enough crushed red pepper in the tomato sauce blanketing the pasta to scare a cold away. Sunny food seasoned with capers and olives, fennel and thyme.

Near Massa Lubrense, the Sorrentine Peninsula's pivot into the Amalfi Drive, is little Santa Maria Annunziata, which Graham Greene loved. In a buttery yellow church on a belvedere that overlooks the opal-streaked violet sea, a member of the Gonzaga family is married. One of the Gonzagas was a pope; another, a duke, was painted by Mantegna. (It amazes me to have been invited to this wedding, which makes me feel like a footnote in history. . . . I met the bride's sister-in-law-to-be on a train.) At the wedding reception, to the noise of an oompah-pah band, we eat peasant food—pigs' feet, *calzoni* (pockets of fried dough stuffed with cheese) with red wine from the slopes of Vesuvius. Then we have *sfogliatelle*, flaky pastry in the shape of a sea shell stuffed with sweetened cheese spiked with chocolate drops, and we drink vintage champagne. Capri twinkles in the near distance. The air smells of jasmine.

In Ravello, the highest point of the Amalfi Drive, I eat every night in a restaurant where everybody knows your name. Netta, the owner and cook, serves gossip with her *tagliatelle* and baby squash; her polenta pancakes stuffed with Parmigiano and *prosciutto; fusilli* with fresh ripe tomatoes and basil; beefsteak with garlic and lemon; an amber *amaro* with flecks of bitter lemon peel.

Pizza Margherita, *a classic, simple preparation of mozzarella cheese, tomato sauce, basil, and olive oil on a pizza crust, sold in the street in front of the Pizza Antica da Michele in Naples.*

Capocolli, *sausages, hanging in the market in Amantea, on the Tyrrhenian coast in Calabria.*

OPPOSITE▶

Fresh fruit stand at the Mercato Lavinai in Naples in June.

View of Pietraferrazzana with the Lago del Sangro in the background.

Bottarga *(also called* ovotarica *in Calabria) is dried and compressed tuna or gray mullet roe, served with lemon, walnuts, black olives, and arugula at the Ristorante Alia in Castrovillari.*

Baskets used for draining cheese at the market in Amantea in Calabria.

On my daughter's saint's day, Netta gives us a bottle of her homemade wine, and a bunch of lemons in a basket of leaves. The lemons perfume our car all the way to Calabria. . . .

Where, in Bagnara, on the Tyrrhenian Sea, we eat swordfish that have journeyed from Arctic waters to spawn in these sun-kissed waters. The way in which they are harvested differs not a whit from the way they were caught before the birth of Christ: harpoonists wait, on extended catwalks twice the length of the peculiar boats, for the warning call of the lookout man, who surveys the sea from a caged platform on top of a forty-foot-tall steel mast. After they are speared and heaved into the boat, the hapless fish—which travel, sacrificial things, in pairs—are carried on the heads of women to the market (their hundreds of pounds of flesh slippery, their needle beaks futile).

My paternal grandfather was born in a hovel in what used to be part of a hunting lodge of Federico Secondo: a little town called Oriolo, in the mountains high above the Ionian Sea, across the peninsula from the Tyrrhenian. . . . Where tables at beach resorts groan with potatoes mixed with shredded goat's cheese and sun-dried tomatoes and oregano; cabbage and *cannellini* beans; *frittata* with cold rice; pasta with tuna and olives and anchovies and red pepper; purple figs and white figs. We drink a faintly lemony *acqua gassata*.

At night my daughter dances in a disco in a ruined castle on the sea, a castle built by Federico.

This is the food of the sun.

Barbara Grizzuti Harrison

Women at a village wash stand in Southern Italy, a familiar sight in this ancient land for thousands of years.

Broom growing in a picturesque valley near Castrovillari in Calabria.

The Via Sacra leading to the Temple of Neptune in the Ancient City of Paestum, in Campania. This temple, now known to have been dedicated to the goddess Hera, is one of the best-preserved Greek temples in Europe.

Fazzoletti Verdi   Green Scarves Lasagne

From the De Marco Family of the Hotel Villa Santa Maria

Serves 10 (3 or 4 *fazzoletti* per serving)

The finished result for fazzoletti verdi, *"green scarves," at the Hotel Villa Santa Maria (recipe right).*

The pasta:

1 pound fresh spinach, washed and
   trimmed
4 cups flour
3 eggs
1 teaspoon salt

The filling:

4 cups ricotta cheese (about
   2 pounds)
3 egg yolks
2 teaspoons salt
1 cup cooked ham cubes (¼-inch
   dice)
¾ cup grated mozzarella cheese
¼ teaspoon grated nutmeg
1 cup freshly grated Parmigiano
   cheese
2 tablespoons chopped parsley

The sauce:

5½ cups tomato sauce (triple the
   recipe on page 218)
5 cups béchamel sauce (5 times the
   recipe on page 126)
1 cup freshly grated Parmigiano
   cheese
2 tablespoons butter, melted, plus
   extra to prepare the pan

Boil the spinach in salted water, drain, allow to cool, squeeze dry, and chop.

Make the pasta dough with the ingredients listed here, following the directions for making pasta on page 247. Add the chopped spinach and salt after beating in the eggs, then knead the dough. Leave to rest for about 15 minutes. Roll out the pasta very thin, and cut with a pastry cutter into approximate 8-inch squares. Put the squares aside for a bit.

Prepare the filling: blend the ricotta cheese with the egg yolks in a bowl. Season with the salt, then add the rest of the ingredients for the filling. Mix everything together well.

Cook the pasta squares in plenty of boiling salted water for a few minutes, several *fazzoletti* at a time. Drain them well.

Preheat the oven to 350°.

Place a few spoonsful of the filling on each pasta square, and then fold over the square from corner to corner, forming a triangle. Butter the bottom of a very large baking pan, pour in some of the tomato and béchamel sauces, and arrange the *fazzoletti* in layers in the dish, repeating the tomato and béchamel sauces and sprinkling Parmigiano cheese between each layer. Pour the melted butter on top. Bake for 45 minutes, or until top is golden brown. Serve hot.   *(Photograph left)*

A Calabrian woman carrying produce on her head at the market in Amantea.

Old olive trees in a field of poppies near Porto di Vasto in the Abruzzi.

Buffalo lounging in the village of Torre Lupara, near Capua in Campania. Their milk is used to make the best mozzarella cheese.

The name of the following traditional preparation for local fish and pasta from Naples means that the linguine *is cooked in the style of the restaurant, but it also plays on the term* cosa nostra, *referring to the Calabrian Mafia. Polipetti are a small variety of octopus that are extremely tender and delicious. They may be hard to find so cuttlefish, or baby octopus, can be substituted.*

Linguine Cosa Nostra   Linguine in the House Style

From Mr. Aversano of Don Salvatore, Naples

Serves 6

2 teaspoons peeled and finely chopped garlic
⅓ cup extra virgin olive oil
2 cups seeded and chopped fresh tomatoes
Salt to taste
1½ pounds *linguine*

½ pound *polipetti* or small octopus, cleaned and cut into pieces
Fish stock or water
6 jumbo prawns, deveined
½ pound mixed shellfish (clams, mussels)
6 large prawns, deveined
½ cup chopped parsley

Cooked seafood to be used in linguine cosa nostra *at Don Salvatore in Naples (recipe left).*

Sauté the garlic in 3 tablespoons olive oil. Add the tomatoes, season with salt, and cook for 10 minutes.

During this time, cook the *linguine* in plenty of boiling salted water until it is *al dente.* When it is done, drain the pasta and put it back in its pot.

In another pan, heat the remaining olive oil until sizzling, add the *polipetti* or octopus pieces, and cook for 3 minutes, until they give off their liquid and turn opaque. Add the octopus and liquid to the tomatoes with about ⅔ cup water, or fish stock if you have it. Place the jumbo prawns in the pan so the tomatoes cover them, and add the clams. Mussels and large prawns should be added 2 minutes later, just before serving.

Turn over the prawns to ensure even cooking, and cover the pan for the last 2 minutes to steam open the shellfish. Add half of the sauce to the pasta, and mix thoroughly. Place this mixture in a large serving dish with the remaining fish and sauce, sprinkle generously with parsley, and serve. *(Photographs above right and opposite page)*

Fresh shellfish for sale at the Mercato Lavinai in Naples.

◄ OPPOSITE
A display of all the ingredients for linguine cosa nostra *before cooking, at Don Salvatore in Naples (recipe above).*

The second stage of preparation for *mines-tra di verdure e pesce* at the Ristorante Alia (recipe right).

*As with most fish soups in Italy, toasted garlic bread (*bruschetta, *recipe page 208) is recommended as an accompaniment here.*

Minestra di Verdure e Pesce   Fish and Vegetable Soup

From Pinuccio and Gaetano Alia at Ristorante Alia, Castrovillari

Serves 4

20 fresh whole jumbo prawns	1 tablespoon chopped parsley
1 medium stalk celery	2 cups seeded and chopped fresh
1 peeled medium carrot and 1 cup	tomatoes
peeled and chopped carrot	3 tablespoons olive oil
1 tablespoon rinsed and chopped	1 diced celery heart
fresh basil leaves	2 cups peeled and chopped potato
¼ teaspoon fennel seeds	2 cups rinsed and chopped zucchini
1 teaspoon chopped fresh thyme,	Salt and pepper to taste
or ¼ teaspoon dried thyme	¼ cup zucchini flowers (optional)

Remove the heads and tails from the prawns. In a medium-sized pot make a stock using the heads, tails, celery stalk, whole carrot, half the basil, fennel, thyme, and parsley, and 2½ cups of water (if prawns are not available with heads on, use tails and shells for the stock). Simmer for 45 minutes, then strain.

When the stock is almost done, sauté the tomatoes in a large frying pan with the oil, then add the 1 cup chopped carrot, the celery heart, potato, and zucchini. Season with salt and pepper, and bring to a boil. Add 2 cups of the strained prawn stock, cover, and continue to simmer. When the vegetables are soft, add the prawns and zucchini flowers if desired, and cook for 5 minutes longer. Garnish with the rest of the basil, fennel, thyme, and parsley, and serve with *bruschetta.*   *(Photographs above left and opposite page)*

Totani in Salsa di Peperoni e Cipolla

Baby Squid in Sweet Pepper and Onion Sauce

From Pinuccio and Gaetano Alia at Ristorante Alia, Castrovillari

Serves 4

⅓ cup peeled and finely chopped	1 cup seeded and chopped fresh
shallots	tomatoes
¼ cup olive oil	1 pound *totani* or baby squid,
1 cup diced green pepper	cleaned and chopped into
1 cup diced yellow pepper	¼-inch rings
1 cup diced red pepper	Salt to taste

Sauté the shallots in 2 tablespoons oil, then add all the peppers and simmer for a few minutes. Add the tomatoes and simmer for 10 minutes.

Then, in another pan, cook the *totani* in the remaining olive oil for a few minutes until they give up their moisture. Drain.

Add the *totani* to the vegetables and season with salt. Cook for about 10 minutes, and serve hot.   *(Photograph left)*

Totani in salsa di peperoni e cipolla *cooking on Gaetano's stove at the Ristorante Alia (recipe right).*

OPPOSITE ▶
Ingredients for minestra di verdure e pesce *at the Ristorante Alia in Castrovillari (recipe above, top).*

Pinuccio Alia, the manager of the Ristorante Alia in the small Calabrian village of Castrovillari, shared his version of a favorite quotation from George Bernard Shaw: "The good things in life are either illegal, immoral, or they make you fat." Pinuccio's brother, Gaetano, rules the kitchen in the restaurant, serving cucina di mamma, *traditional Calabrian home cooking, updated for today's palate. The Alia brothers recommend serving this fish salad the day after you have made it as an antipasto, or between a first course and a sturdy meat course.*

Insalata di Baccalà Crudo   Raw Codfish Salad

From Pinuccio and Gaetano Alia at Ristorante Alia, Castrovillari

Serves 4

1½ pounds fresh rock cod	½ cup rinsed and chopped fresh
¼ cup fresh lemon juice	mint leaves
¼ cup olive oil	⅓ cup peeled and chopped onion
1 teaspoon cayenne pepper	Salt and pepper to taste
½ cup rinsed and chopped fresh	
basil leaves	

Crates of baccalà, *salted codfish, at the market in Amantea on the Tyrrhenian coast in Calabria.*

Slice the cod about ½ inch thick, following the vein. Arrange the slices in a dish. Pour the lemon juice over the fish, and leave for 30 minutes in the refrigerator. Next, pour on the oil, sprinkle the cayenne pepper over the fish, and let marinate for 10 minutes. Sprinkle on the basil, mint, and onion. Turn the fish 2 or 3 times, at 20-minute intervals, then put it in the refrigerator to sit overnight. Season with salt and pepper before serving.
(Photograph opposite page)

This soufflé should be served as a first course as soon as it comes out of the oven.

Flan di Zucchini   Zucchini Soufflé

From Pinuccio and Gaetano Alia at Ristorante Alia, Castrovillari

Serves 6

3 cups rinsed and chopped zucchini	⅛ teaspoon grated nutmeg
4 eggs, separated	1 teaspoon salt
½ cup grated Parmigiano cheese	3 tablespoons butter

Preheat the oven to 350°.
Blanch the zucchini in boiling salted water for a minute. Drain and purée in a food processor or blender. Drain well again. In a large bowl, beat the egg yolks with the Parmigiano cheese and nutmeg, and stir in the zucchini and the salt. In another bowl, beat the egg whites until stiff; fold them into the zucchini mixture.

Grease 6 individual ramekins or a baking dish with the butter, fill with the zucchini mixture, and bake for about 25 minutes, or until crusty and puffed on top.

◄ OPPOSITE
The ingredients and finished result for insalata di baccalà crudo *at the Ristorante Alia in Castrovillari (recipe above, top).*

Brodetto di pesce *(recipe right) ready to be served at Il Corsaro with* bruschetta, *toasted bread soaked in olive oil and rubbed with garlic (recipe page 208).*

Serve this fish soup hot with slices of toasted garlic bread (bruschetta, recipe page 208).

Brodetto di Pesce alla Donna Lina   Lina's Fish Soup

From Mr. and Mrs. Crisci of Ristorante Il Corsaro, Porto di Vasto

Serves 4

5 tablespoons olive oil	1 cup diced green pepper
2 teaspoons peeled and finely chopped garlic	2 pounds assorted fish fillets (red mullet, cod, and the like), cut into pieces
½ cup chopped parsley	
One 1-pound can plum tomatoes, roughly chopped, with liquid	Salt to taste
	Cayenne pepper to taste

Pour the oil into a large pan, add the chopped garlic and parsley, and sauté lightly; then add the chopped tomatoes with their liquid and the green pepper, and cook for about 10 minutes.

Pour a layer of this tomato sauce on the bottom of a large pot, and arrange the fish pieces in layers in the pot according to their cooking times, placing the most delicate fish at the top. Pour in the remaining tomato sauce, salt to taste, cover, and simmer gently for half an hour. Serve the soup with *bruschetta,* and a dusting of cayenne pepper to taste.
(Photographs left and opposite page)

Sardine alle Scapece   Sardines in Spicy Sauce

From the Ristorante Alfonso a Mare, Praiano

Serves 4

2 pounds fresh cleaned sardines (gutted, heads and backbones removed; weighed after cleaning)	⅔ cup vinegar
	1 cup rinsed and chopped fresh mint leaves, plus extra for garnish
2 tablespoons fresh lemon juice	6 teaspoons peeled and finely chopped garlic
Salt to taste	
½ cup flour	1 teaspoon seeded and finely chopped serrano chile pepper
¼ cup olive oil, plus extra for garnish	
2 medium onions, peeled and cut into thick rings	

Soak the sardines in a shallow bowl in the lemon juice, a pinch of salt, and water to cover for about half an hour to eliminate their strong flavor. Wash and dry them, then coat them with flour.

Cook the sardines in 2 tablespoons olive oil in a large frying pan over medium heat, about 2 minutes per side. When they are done, drain them on paper towels and sprinkle with salt.

Sauté the onion rings in the remaining olive oil. When they are about half tender, carefully add the vinegar, and cook until it nearly evaporates. Add the chopped mint, garlic, and chile pepper, and continue cooking until the onions are soft.

Arrange the sardines in a serving dish and cover them with the onion sauce. Let them sit in the refrigerator for about half a day before serving. Add some fresh mint and olive oil when ready to serve.

OPPOSITE PAGE ▶
An array of ingredients for brodetto di pesce *(recipe above right). Local specialties shown here at Il Corsaro include* nasello, cappone, triglie, scorfano, merluzzo, calamaretti, cicala di mare, and scampi, *but practically any fish available can be used.*

Mr. Esposito, the pastry cook at the Cappuccini Convento in Amalfi, says pastiera *is even better eaten a day after it has been made (in which case it should be refrigerated overnight).*

Pastiera   Neapolitan Easter Cake

From Mr. Aiello of the Ristorante Cappuccini Convento, Amalfi

Serves 8

A classic view of Amalfi, looking down from the Ristorante Cappuccini Convento in the hills above town.

The *pasta frolla* (short crust):

2 cups white flour
⅔ cup sugar
8 tablespoons (1 stick) unsalted butter, softened, plus extra to prepare the pan
3 egg yolks
1 whole egg
1 tablespoon grated lemon or orange peel
Pinch of salt

The filling:

2 cups ricotta cheese (about 1 pound)

½ cup plus 2 tablespoons sugar
3 eggs, separated (each yolk and white in different containers), at room temperature
¼ teaspoon cinnamon, plus a pinch for the milk
⅓ cup chopped candied orange or citrus peel
2 tablespoons fresh lemon juice
½ teaspoon grated lemon peel
¼ cup rum, or 1 teaspoon vanilla
2 cups milk
¼ pound *vermicelli* or *capellini* pasta
Pinch of salt

Confectioners' sugar for decoration

To make the crust, sift the flour and make a mound of it on your work surface, or in a large bowl. Add ⅔ cup sugar, then make a well in the mound and add the soft butter. Lightly beat the egg yolks and whole egg together and put them in the well. Continue to beat the eggs with a fork, gradually working in the dry ingredients until all are well mixed. Add the grated lemon or orange peel and a pinch of salt, and work with your hands until the ingredients form a buttery, soft dough. Shape it into a ball, wrap in plastic wrap, and chill in the refrigerator for about 30 minutes.

Preheat the oven to 400°.

For the filling, put the ricotta in a large bowl and beat until smooth. Add ½ cup of sugar and stir in the 3 egg yolks 1 at a time, until well blended. Add ¼ teaspoon cinnamon, the candied peel, the lemon juice and grated lemon peel, and the rum. In a separate bowl, whip 2 egg whites with 1 tablespoon of sugar until stiff, and fold into the ricotta/egg mixture.

Boil the milk in a small pot and toss in the pasta. Simmer gently with a pinch of salt, pinch of cinnamon, and 1 tablespoon of sugar until all the milk has been absorbed. Let cool. Finally, fold the cooked pasta into the ricotta/egg mixture.

Flour your work area and roll out ⅔ of the pastry into a 12-inch round. Place it in the bottom of a buttered 10-inch cake or springform pan, spreading it carefully along the bottom of the pan and around the sides, and pierce it a few times with a fork. Pour in the ricotta/egg mixture. Reflour the work surface and roll out the rest of the *pasta frolla*, cut it into long thin strips, and place them lattice fashion on top of the *pastiera*. Brush with a bit of the third, slightly beaten egg white.

Reduce the heat to 375° and bake the cake for 1 hour or a few minutes longer, until the lattice on top is nicely toasted and cooked through. Cool before serving. Dust with confectioners' sugar.
(Photograph opposite page)

◄ OPPOSITE PAGE
Pastiera napoletana, *Neapolitan Easter cake, the gastronomic symbol of Naples, shown here at the Ristorante Cappuccini Convento in Amalfi (recipe left).*

The same view of Amalfi, from the balcony of the Ristorante Cappuccini Convento, at night.

Francesca Fiori making orecchiette *with her daughter in the street, in the old town of Bari.*

Salsiccia sott'olio piccante, *sausage preserved in oil, served with olives and bread at the Ristorante da Mario in Matera. Sausages are a distinctive feature of Basilicatan cuisine.*

Trays of fresh pasta at the Ristorante Panoramico in Castro Marina, on the bottom of Italy's "heel" in Apulia: orecchiette, *the most widely made pasta in this region;* maccheroncini; *and* ravioli.

◄ OVERLEAF
View across the valley to the hill town of Atena Lucana, near the border between Campania and Basilicata.

VIII. *Apulia/Basilicata*

IT IS MY PLEASURE to tell you about Apulia, my home, which lies on the southeastern edge of the Italian peninsula, a land at once barren and beautiful, bordered by the gentle Ionian Sea and the more lively Adriatic. I would also like to say something about the Apulians, a tenacious people dedicated to land and sea, trade and farming. And I would like to tell you about Basilicata, enclosed within its high borders like Sleeping Beauty awaiting the prince. We will travel along a path connecting aromas, flavors, and moods; from this journey I hope that you will gain an understanding of the southerner's soul.

Apulia (the name is Latin) became a country in 1043. Today, its roughly 7740 square miles support a population of about four million. The landscape is variously flat, hilly, or—rarely—mountainous. Apulia's inhabitants are at one with the land, as are their customs and traditions. Apulian food is part of this union, and the safeguarding of certain culinary traditions here is as important as the conservation of the landscape, monuments, and works of art.

This barren region, particularly the hilly and farming areas, preserves its customs within the fissures of dry land and scorched rock and in the cracked surfaces of twisted trees beaten by the implacable northwest wind, which can bend even the indomitable olive tree in agony.

Olives and olive oil have always been the wealth of Apulia. The oil comes from a variety of producers all over the region, with many different levels of quality, the only common denominator being abundance. The making of holy oil for the lamps used to give thanks for healing, and in the candles lit for souls in purgatory, has always accompanied the making of young, green, pungent olive oil, whose first pressing is welcomed with singing and dancing. Celebrations accompany the wheat harvest as well, when sheaves are tied together and placed under the arches of great rustic doors to bring fertility and prosperity to those living within.

Oil and wheat, staples of this region, stand at the beginning and end of a long chain of indigenous foods that are genuine, simple, and sincere, as are the Apulians themselves. Here the oil is wedded with such products of the earth as eggplant, artichokes, sweet peppers, mushrooms, sweet onions, and tomatoes, giving life to the area's inhabitants while supplying the rest of the world with elements of the Mediterranean diet our forefathers discovered.

The provident nature of Apulia is evident in its many wheat products, such as flour, cereals, pastas, *focaccie, taralli* (recipe page 210), *friselle,* and biscuits. Even now, in some villages of inland Apulia, women continue the tradition of circulating the yeast for making bread, and it is still possible to find wooden or metal seals bearing the monogram or distinctive family mark that is stamped on loaves before baking. In certain corners of the region, marked by cobblestone streets and stone steps whitened by bleach and women's hard work, it is said that bread is the providence of God and must never be played with or thrown away. Those who waste bread will be condemned to as many years in purgatory as the number of crumbs wasted and will have to pick those crumbs up, one by one, with their eyelids. "Even placing a loaf upside-down is not allowed," women dressed in black explain, sitting under arches along narrow streets, singing as they roll their *orecchiette* (recipe for serving *orecchiette*, page 213) and corkscrew pastas, as pots indoors bubble with *ragù* sauce. "It would be like turning one's face away from Christ." Continuing by them, one can hear more bubbling pots, perhaps containing beans, which are still cooked on the hearth or in wood-burning stoves, in places where pressure cookers and microwave ovens are unknown. Legumes, another recently rediscovered element of Mediterranean cuisine, were the mainstay of the peasant diet for decades. Working far from their homes, peasant cooks would leave beans to simmer all day, returning in the evening to eat the purée. They say that Hercules acquired the strength for his mythical undertakings from the purée of fava beans, which, combined with fresh sweet chicory or Swiss chard is served as a delicacy today (*'Ncapriata*, recipe page 208).

Another enduring ritual of Apulia is that performed during the annual bottling of fresh tomato sauce. This tradition continues in the courtyards of the old city centers, in Bari and other towns large and small. A short distance from the chaotic traffic jams and frenetic pace of contemporary life, one may find whole families and flocks of neighbors brought together by this custom. The first day, perhaps the hottest and muggiest day in August, begins with the selection of the tomatoes, which, according to the older women, must be red, ripe, and undamaged. After the tomatoes have been chopped and boiled, they are sieved through food mills by the youngest participants, and then everyone, young and old, men and women, joins forces to pour the sauce into carefully washed bottles, adding a few basil leaves so that some of the flavors and colors of the summer will be preserved for the winter. Airtight bottle caps are used today, but at one time corks were used, and some still prefer them. The boiling or sterilization of the bottles occurs at sunset, and everyone, warm and content, sits and enjoys the cool evening air. If one of the bottles bursts while boiling, making a cracking sound like fireworks, it is considered a sign of good luck and is greeted with an explosion of contagious laughter.

The magic and charm of Apulia are a mixture of ancient and modern, sacred and profane, religion and paganism, combined so judiciously that it is hard to see where one ends and the other begins. This is why on some small streets on the Gargano Promontory, people still ride donkeys while planes speed overhead, and why a single field can be shared by telephone poles, beets, fennel, and grazing herds. Similarly, processions and carnival parades, the rites for rain or a good harvest, will hold up traffic and cause amazement. Apulia is like that: you can cross the street and face an ancient world, knowing that the realm of modern technology is right behind you. Here the two worlds are happily and quietly hinged together, since one can find in each what the other lacks, or its opposite.

Winemaking is the occasion for further rituals, from the harvest to the pressing of the grapes to the

A shepherd of the Gargano Promontory
in Apulia, with a baby lamb born one
hour before, near Monte Sant'Angelo.

OPPOSITE ▶
*Basilicata is known for the quality of its
dairy products, especially the fresh cheeses.
Here, with a ricotta cheese on the plate, is
a variety of pecorino (sheep's milk)
cheeses, at different stages of
preparation.*

bottling, including a feast from which emanates the odor of must, a perfume unique to Apulia. The area's wines—like the genuine, sincere, and robust Dauni that go well with starchy foods (the Gargano area is known as the granary of Italy), red meat, savory game, and fresh fish—have a sunny taste. Cerasuoli wines are delicate and dry, while Salento whites are dry and brilliant, with a fresh bouquet, and go well with foods descended from the ancient Greeks. (It seems that the Greeks were given sumptuous Archestrato wine by Salentine cooks and were thus released from the monotony of Spartan discipline to cultivate gentler ways and customs.) The wines of the Taranto area range from the ruby-colored reds to sweet wines, from primitive wines to the slightly sparkling ones of the Valle d'Itria. These wines are an excellent complement to the seafood from the area around Taranto, which was founded, according to legend, by the Spartan hero Falanto and the adventurous commander Taras, born of the union between Neptune and a nymph.

I should mention the Apulians' devotion to traditional food, particularly the meals eaten at Christmas, Easter, and other holidays, year after year. I am referring, for example, to the custom of serving thirteen courses—no more, no less—on Christmas Eve; to the *scarcelle* that a fiancée prepares for her beau at Easter; to the *frappe* made for the feast of Saint Joseph; and to the sweet *taralli* made for the Good Friday procession. For the people of this place, as for the people of every land, food is memory, tradition, a body of ancestral tastes that must be passed on to younger generations. This cuisine is like the weapon given by the ancient warrior to his first-born son, like the wedding veil passed on from mother to daughter, like family jewels. This is a message to treasure, just as you would cherish the aroma of Apulian vegetables *parmigiana*; rice, potato, and mussel casserole; *ragù* meat sauces simmered for hours; fresh, multicolored salads; sensuous, delectable seafood; or ricotta eaten warm right out of a reed basket.

This should be your lasting image of Apulia, a place that has accepted the passage of time but has never really changed: clusters of hot peppers and baby tomatoes hanging outside windows as they have for centuries, next to long garlic braids used during the winter, but also intended to ward off the evil eye.

A woman pruning leaves from a grapevine near Martina Franca in Apulia.

An avenue of umbrella pines near San Pancrazio in Apulia.

◄ OPPOSITE
A man carrying poppies on his bike on the road to Casamassima, near Bari in Apulia.

Zuppa del pescatore, *ready to cook at the Ristorante Panoramico, in the hotel of the same name in Castro Marina, Apulia. The restaurant keeps its own fishing boat, to ensure a fresh catch. This version of fish soup includes lobster, mussels, clams, a* pagello *(sea bream), onion, garlic, tomatoes, potatoes, parsley, and oregano.*

Some controversy surrounds the origin of the name Basilicata. It may derive from a tenth-century Byzantine administrator from the Basilica of Acerenza, whose bishop exercised jurisdiction over the territory. What is certain is that the present borders of the region—sometimes called Lucania—are similar to what they were according to a document of 1277, when the area encompassed 148 towns, to which Matera was added in 1663, becoming the region's capital.

To trace the history, art, and folklore of the region, as well as its most traditional foods and ways of preparing them, is a difficult task. The cuisine of Basilicata, while perhaps not strikingly unique, and though similar in certain ways to the cuisines of Apulia and Calabria, nevertheless has its particular flavors. They are difficult to describe; their secrets may lie in alchemies preserved somewhere in the region's ragged cliffs and gorges. Flavors like those of the *maccheroni a ferretti*, strips of pasta perforated with thin wires, impossible to find elsewhere; or the *stivaletti*, a variant of the *orecchiette* of Apulia; or the soup of Maratea, a flavorful dish made from legumes, onions, potatoes, and various garden vegetables—not all, however, known and revealed! Game hunting, a practice dating back to the time of the lords of Lagopesole, Tricarico, Venosa, Lagonegro, Melfi, and Lavello and originally intended to pass the time between an invasion and a holy crusade or an expedition to Naples to plot conspiracies, still lives on. Now, though, plots are only hatched between father and son and concern the secrets of tenderizing meat and removing the gamy odors of the woods from it. Woodcocks, quails, partridges, hares, and even wild boar may all be had here, roasted in ovens, braised, or cooked in nets or in pots. The eels of Lake Monticchio and the trout of the Sirino are equally delicious.

You see, then, that in Basilicata as in Apulia, the flavors of the foods derive from the mixture of the air, earth, and sun and from the toil of all those who work the land, set out to sea, gather fruit, and store for leaner times. Even the products of the garden here carry the names of their places of origin, so as not to be confused with one another. One refers to the fennel of Potenza or Melfi, the *tabacchini* beans of Pignola, the *poverelli* beans of Lauria, the fava beans of Lavello, the chickpeas of Matera, the sweet peppers of Senise.

Zuppa del pescatore, *ready to be served at the Hotel Panoramico in Castro Marina.*

In Molfetta, on the Adriatic coast of Apulia between Bari and Trani, a view beyond the fishing boats in the bay to the thirteenth-century duomo vecchio, *the old cathedral.*

Antonio di Pace opening sea urchins at the fish market in Porto Cesareo, on the Gulf of Taranto in Apulia.

This land seems so closed, but eventually it opens its heart even to the foreigner, leading him gently to love its places and people and to comprehend the true causes of an isolation freely chosen, as a means to resist the passage of time and impact of history. Basilicata is like its foodstuffs, hard on the outside and soft within—like its *butirri* (small *provola* cheeses with the soul of butter) or *pezzotti* (sweet pastry stuffed with honey and nuts) or the sweet chestnuts of Vulture, which are jealously protected by their sharply pointed outer shells and then, once opened, just as generously bestowed. Even the wines of Basilicata mirror the character of its inhabitants. They include savory, full-bodied Aglianico from the area of Vulture, with its brilliant garnet color, and equally fine white wines such as Asprino di Ruoti, Malvasia di Rapolla, Moscato di Melfi, Barile, Rapolla, Maschito, and Ripacandida.

The ancient castles of Basilicata and the lookout towers along the coast of Apulia still stand as they have through the centuries. On a clear day, one can almost imagine bold sentries calling to each other from tower to tower, in secret code, colorful stories of times past, or of the more tangible present; stories with overtones of suffering and passion, and of rites and traditions which they have witnessed, and have guarded, for so long.

And now our voyage is truly at an end.

Paola Pettini

Traditional mussel farming near Taranto in Apulia.

Centuries-old olive trees near Torre Canne, on the Adriatic coast of Apulia between Bari and Brindisi.

Mysterious buildings called trulli, *in a field near Ceglie Messapico, outside of Martina Franca in what is known as the "Trulli District" in Apulia. These strange, whitewashed dry-stone domed houses show traces of ancient Saracen and Christian civilizations.*

A still life of bread, oil, and tomatoes in preparation for one of the most basic of Italian dishes, bruschetta *(recipe right).*

OPPOSITE PAGE ▶
Bruschetta *shown cooked with its basic ingredients at the Ristorante da Mario in Matera, the provincial capital of Basilicata (similar recipe, right, from Paola Pettini).*

Outside a colorfully painted farmhouse near Matera in Basilicata, garlic, drying tomatoes, and basil distill the very essence of Italy.

Bruschetta *is found all over Italy, from Tuscany to Apulia. Its simplicity leaves nothing to hide behind. The secret of a successful preparation of this Apulian version is to find the freshest tomatoes, the hardiest bread (homemade, if possible), and the purest olive oil, preferably imported from Italy.*

In Apulia this bruschetta *would be served as an appetizer. It is recommended as an accompaniment to the recipes for fish soup on pages 153, 186, and 190. When serving* bruschetta *as a side dish, you may want to leave off the tomatoes, simply dousing the bread in olive oil and then rubbing it with garlic.*

Bruschetta   Toasted Bread with Tomatoes

From Paola Pettini of Bari

Serves 4

One 8-ounce loaf Italian or French bread cut into 8 slices	2 large, ripe tomatoes, cut into thick slices
1 clove garlic, peeled and cut in half	Salt and pepper to taste
½ cup olive oil	Fresh oregano

Arrange the bread slices on a baking rack and toast them in a moderate oven until browned on both sides. When the bread is toasted, place the slices on a large dish and quickly rub the cut side of the garlic clove on 1 side of each slice. Pour 1 tablespoon of olive oil on top of each side rubbed with garlic. Distribute the tomatoes evenly among the bread slices, then sprinkle with salt, pepper, and fresh oregano. Pouring on another generous amount of oil at the end is optional. Try to serve hot.
(Photographs left and opposite page)

'Ncapriata *is Apulian dialect for* fave e cicoria, *beans and chicory, today eaten as a side dish. It is one of the most ancient dishes of the Mediterranean region, dating back to the pharaohs (in fact, it is still popular in Egypt).*

'Ncapriata   Purée of Broad Beans with Chicory

From Paola Pettini of Bari

Serves 4

1½ cups dried *fave* (broad beans)	1 head chicory, approximately 1 pound
Salt to taste	
¼ cup extra virgin olive oil, plus extra for the chicory	

Clean and rinse the *fave* well. Cover them with water and soak overnight.

Remove the outer dark shells and rinse the beans. Put them in a pot, add enough water to cover, and start cooking. As soon as they reach a boil, reduce the heat and, stirring occasionally, cook over low heat until the *fave* can be easily mashed (about 1 hour). Turn off the heat, season with salt, and leave for 30 minutes.

Put the *fave* through a food mill or food processor, blend to a purée, and then beat in the olive oil.

Wash, trim, and cook the chicory separately in boiling salted water until tender, about 3 to 5 minutes, and drain. Serve the *fave* with the chicory, with olive oil to dress the chicory.

Typical breads of Apulia at La Forneria in Martina Franca, top to bottom: frise, taralli *(recipe right), and* focacciete.

Taralli *are unsweetened biscuits (from the old French* bis cuits, *meaning "cooked twice"), to be dunked in or eaten with wine as a snack. The flavoring of* taralli *varies; in Bari they are left plain; in Taranto, they taste of fennel; and in Brindisi and Lecce, they are well peppered. Here Paola Pettini shares a recipe in the Taranto style.*

Taralli Scaldatelli   Taralli Bread

From Paola Pettini of Bari

For 3 dozen *taralli*

3 cups all-purpose flour	½ cup olive oil, warmed, plus extra
1 package dry yeast	to prepare the baking sheet
1 tablespoon fennel seeds	¾ cup dry white wine, warmed

Mix the flour with the yeast and the fennel seeds. Fold in the oil and wine, which must both be warm. Turn the dough out onto a floured work surface and knead it well until it is smooth and firm. Leave the dough to rest for 10 minutes.

Take some dough and roll it out with your hands into a rope ¼ inch in diameter. Cut the rope into 2-inch lengths, form each into a ring, and press the ends to seal them together. Continue this procedure until you have used up all the dough.

Preheat the oven to 375°. Place a large pot filled with salted water on high heat to boil.

Drop the *taralli* into the boiling salted water. When they come to the surface, lift the *taralli* out with a slotted spoon. Allow them to dry thoroughly on a dishcloth. Bake the *taralli* on a large oiled baking sheet for 15 to 20 minutes. Serve warm or cool.   *(Photograph left)*

1. *Sea urchins, oysters, and mussels on sale at the Interlalanza Sunday market in Bari.*

2. *Red and yellow peppers at the Mercato di via Nicolai in Bari.*

3. *Squid in baskets at the Interlalanza market in Bari.*

4. *Various local cheeses at the Casa del Latticino in Avigliano, near Potenza in Basilicata, top to bottom:* ricotta *in molds,* trecciette, *and* mozzarelle.

5. *School children in uniform in Alberobello, the capital of the Trulli District in Apulia.*

6. *Eggplant slices cooked directly on the stove at the Ristorante Panoramico in Castro Marina in Apulia.*

7. *Drying tomatoes on a balcony in the south of Italy.*

8. *Fishing boats in the harbor in Castro Marina, on the Ionian Sea.*

9. *Fresh sardines at the Mercato di via Nicolai in Bari.*

1

2

3

4

5

6

7

8

9

Orecchiette, *"little ears,"* are the most symbolic pasta of Apulia, a region famed for its pasta consumption. An orecchietta *looks like a small shell, and is made by simple pressure of the thumb on small disks cut from a thick stick of dough. The resulting hollow traps whatever sauce is used to flavor the pasta.*

Orecchiette e Cime di Rapa

Orecchiette with Turnip Greens

From Paola Pettini of Bari

Serves 6

2 pounds *cime di rapa* (turnip greens)
1 pound dried *orecchiette*
¼ cup salt, plus extra to taste
12 anchovy fillets packed in oil

4 teaspoons peeled and coarsely chopped garlic
¼ cup olive oil
½ teaspoon red pepper flakes, plus extra to taste

Clean the *cime*, remove the stems, and use only the most tender leaves and tops. Wash the greens well, and allow to drip dry.

Cook the *orecchiette* in plenty of boiling water with ¼ cup salt, following the directions on the box. 2 minutes before they are done, add the greens to the pot, and stir.

While the pasta is cooking, rinse the anchovies well, and pat the fillets dry. In a saucepan, sauté the garlic in the olive oil with the red pepper flakes, then add the anchovies and cook for a few minutes over low heat, mashing the anchovies with a spoon until they dissolve.

Drain the pasta and greens when the pasta is *al dente*. Remove the garlic from the sauce, and pour the sauce over the *orecchiette*. Season with more salt and red pepper flakes to taste, and serve very hot.
(Photograph of orecchiette, *above right)*

Orecchiette *with ingredients for a plain tomato sauce at the Trattoria delle Ruote near Martina Franca (recipe for serving* orecchiette, *left).*

A typical afternoon street scene in Martina Franca.

◄ OPPOSITE
Antipasti *at the Trattoria delle Ruote near Martina Franca, a restaurant specializing in the home cooking of Apulia. Shown are pickled artichokes, carrots, zucchini, yellow peppers, onions, peas, and green beans, with* pancetta *and* capocollo *(two cured meats), and some fresh bread.*

Ingredients for frittata di asparagi *(recipe right), shown with a loaf of* focaccia, *in this case a pepperbread, at the Ristorante Il Fusillo. Either oil or butter, or both, can be used in this recipe.*

Serve this omelet as a lunch or light dinner, with fresh bread.

Frittata di Asparagi   Wild Asparagus Omelet

From Maria Summa, manager of the Ristorante Il Fusillo, Avigliano

Serves 2

One ½-pound bunch wild asparagus, or 1 pound domestic asparagus	Salt and freshly grated pepper to taste
4 eggs	1 tablespoon olive oil
¼ cup grated *pecorino* or Romano cheese	

Wild asparagus (*asparagi di campo,* "from the field") are so thin and tender they do not need to be cooked before being added to the omelet. Simply wash them; there is no need to cut them. If you are using domestic asparagus, cut the tips including 1 inch from the stalk, and cook them in boiling salted water for 4 minutes. Drain, and proceed with the recipe. You can use the top 2 inches of the domestic asparagus stalk as well—just cut this part into 1-inch lengths and blanch along with the tips.

In a bowl, beat the eggs well and mix in the asparagus, cheese, and salt and pepper to taste. Heat the olive oil in a skillet or omelet pan, and pour in the egg mixture. As soon as the bottom is solidified and browned, turn the *frittata* over, and cook the second side to a golden brown. *(Photographs left and opposite page)*

Cozze gratinate prepared to be cooked at the Ristorante Panoramico in Castro Marina (similar recipe, right, from Paola Pettini).

Cozze Gratinate   Mussels au Gratin

From Paola Pettini of Bari

Serves 6

3 pounds mussels in their shells	¼ teaspoon salt
½ cup dried breadcrumbs	½ teaspoon pepper
¼ cup chopped parsley	½ cup olive oil
2 teaspoons peeled and finely chopped garlic	

Preheat the oven to 375°.

Scrub and clean the mussels thoroughly. Put them in a heavy pan over fairly high heat with ¾ inch of water in the bottom, and cook, covered, just until they open. Strain the liquid, saving ¼ cup. Remove the empty top shell of each mussel, and place the mussels in their half-shells in a baking dish.

Mix the breadcrumbs with the mussel liquid, the parsley, the chopped garlic, the salt and pepper, and ¼ cup of the olive oil. Sprinkle this mixture generously over the mussels. Pour the rest of the oil over the mussels, heat them in the oven for 10 minutes, and serve.   *(Photograph left)*

OPPOSITE▶

Frittata di asparagi ready to be served with focaccia *at the Ristorante Il Fusillo in the Gala Hotel in Avigliano (recipe above, top).*

*Townspeople in the shade at the entrance
to the castle in Miglionico, south of
Matera in Basilicata.*

The ingredients and preparation for fusilli al ragù, *also called* braciole al ragù, *at the Ristorante Il Fusillo in the Gala Hotel in Avigliano, outside of Potenza (recipe right). The packets of beef or veal are cooked in what becomes the sauce for the pasta, and then the meat packets, called* involtini, *are served as the second course. These* fusilli *were hand-made by Mrs. Pierina Zaccagnino.*

Fusilli *is wire-thin pasta, rolled into a spiral with the aid of a spit. The dough is the simplest combination possible, durum wheat and water. Here the* fusilli *are served with a mild meat sauce.*

Fusilli al Ragù   Fusilli Pasta with Meat Sauce

From Maria Summa, manager of the Ristorante Il Fusillo, Avigliano

Serves 4

2 pounds top or bottom round
 roast, cut into 8 thin slices
3 teaspoons peeled and finely
 chopped garlic
1½ cups peeled and finely chopped
 onion
2 cups peeled and finely chopped
 carrot
¼ cup finely chopped parsley
¼ cup grated *pecorino* or *provolone*
 cheese
¼ cup dried breadcrumbs

1 tablespoon salt
2 teaspoons pepper
Flour (optional)
2 tablespoons olive oil
3 ounces lean *pancetta*, chopped
 to yield ¾ cup
One 28-ounce can plum tomatoes,
 drained and finely chopped or put
 through a food mill
1 cup dry red or white wine
1 pound *fusilli*

Pound the meat slices between pieces of wax paper to make them even thinner and more tender.

In a bowl, mix together half the chopped garlic and onion (saving the other half of each for the sauce), and the carrot, parsley, cheese, breadcrumbs, and 1 teaspoon each salt and pepper. Sprinkle each slice of meat with ¼ teaspoon salt and ⅛ teaspoon pepper, and put 3 tablespoons of the stuffing mixture in the middle of each slice of meat. Roll each slice from 1 corner to its opposite corner on the diagonal, making as long a roll as possible, then fold over the ends, 1 at a time, toward the middle of the roll until they slightly overlap, making a packet that you can either skewer with a toothpick or tie with cotton thread to hold shut during cooking. (Some cooks like to dust the packets with flour at this stage.)

In a large skillet, sauté the packets *(involtini)* in the olive oil, turning them until they are brown all over. When they are done, remove them from the oil, but leave the oil in the pan.

Sauté the chopped *pancetta* in the oil with the remaining onion and garlic over low heat until the onion is soft. Stir frequently and be careful not to burn the garlic. Then add the tomatoes and the wine, and put the *involtini* back in. The liquid in the pan should just cover the meat; if it does not, add some hot water. Bring to the boil, cover, reduce the heat, and simmer for about 2 hours, stirring occasionally, until the sauce has been reduced and concentrated, and the meat is very tender.

When the meat is about done, cook the *fusilli* in plenty of boiling salted water until *al dente*, and then drain. Dress the *fusilli* with the meat sauce, but save a little sauce to go with the *involtini*, which are served as a second course. Remember to remove the thread, if you used it, before serving the meat, 2 packets per serving.   *(Photograph left)*

A man pruning an olive tree in May near Bitritto, outside of Bari in Apulia.

These bread balls can be eaten plain right after they are fried, or they can be cooked briefly in tomato sauce just to flavor, and served with sautéed artichoke hearts (for the preparation of artichokes, see recipe on page 126).

Polpette di Pane   Bread Balls

From Paola Pettini of Bari

For 2 dozen *polpette*

The *polpette*:
5 eggs
¼ cup chopped parsley
1 teaspoon peeled and chopped
   garlic
1 teaspoon salt
½ teaspoon pepper
½ cup freshly grated Parmigiano
   or Romano cheese
3 cups dried white breadcrumbs

Vegetable oil for frying the *polpette*

To serve:

Tomato sauce (preparation follows)
6 artichoke hearts, thinly sliced
2 tablespoons olive oil
2 teaspoons peeled and finely
   chopped garlic
¼ cup chopped parsley

Mix all of the ingredients for the *polpette* together in a bowl until you have a firm mixture. Make balls the size of walnuts with the mixture, and fry them until golden in medium-hot oil. Drain and serve, or cook lightly in tomato sauce (recipe below). Sauté the artichokes in the olive oil with chopped garlic and parsley for 10 minutes, and serve with the *polpette*, if desired.

For 2 cups tomato sauce:

2 tablespoons olive oil
1 garlic clove, peeled and cut in half
One 28-ounce can plum tomatoes,

coarsely chopped, with liquid
1 tablespoon chopped parsley
Salt to taste

Heat the olive oil in a medium-sized skillet and cook the garlic in it until golden; then discard the garlic. Add the chopped tomatoes to the skillet with their liquid and simmer for about 10 minutes, stirring occasionally, until the sauce is slightly thickened. Add the chopped parsley, season with salt, remove from the heat, and serve.

One of the best-known desserts of Basilicata, fichi secchi ammandorlati, at the Ristorante da Mario in Matera (recipe right). Here they are garnished with laurel leaves.

Fichi Secchi Ammandorlati
Dried Figs Stuffed with Almonds

From the Ristorante da Mario, Matera

Serves 4

12 dried figs
¼ cup blanched and finely chopped
   almonds

¼ cup honey, plus extra for garnish
¼ teaspoon fennel seeds

If the figs are very dry and hard, soak them in water for 2 hours.

Preheat the oven to 300°. Incise the figs with a cross-shaped cut ½ inch from the bottom of each fig. Combine the almonds, honey, and fennel seeds in a small mixing bowl. Fill the incision in the figs with this mixture, and press the top of the fig down to close the incision. Drizzle more honey over the figs, and bake for 20 minutes. Serve warm.   *(Photograph left)*

At the Rinaldi Giuseppe bakery shop in Monte Sant'Angelo, on the Gargano Promontory in Apulia.

Young women gathering straw after the harvest on a massena, *a large farm, near Martina Franca in Apulia.*

The interior of the Museum Room at the Albergo Sacchi, a day trip from the town of Nuoro, on Monte Ortobene in Sardinia. This small building located away from the main hotel is kept with a traditional interior and used for special occasions. Here the proprietors display some local foods: a smoked ham hangs on the wall; carta di musica bread and a variety of pecorino cheeses are in the foreground.

The Temple of Concord at sunset, in Agrigento on the southern coast of Sicily.

◄ OVERLEAF
A bustling scene at the Vucciria market in Palermo, the capital and chief seaport of Sicily. The name means literally "the noisy market."

IX. *Sicily/Sardinia*

For MORE THAN 2,500 YEARS, contrast and diversity have found an enduring home in Sicily. In its strategic position between Europe and Africa, Sicily was one of the great melting pots of the ancient world, home at one time to every great civilization in the Mediterranean: Greek and Roman, Arab and Norman, and finally French, Spanish, and Italian. (It has, in fact, been part of Italy only a little over a hundred years.) Something of all of these peoples has been absorbed in the rich tapestry that makes up Sicilian life: its customs, its language, and its food.

A symbiosis of traditions is fundamental to Sicilian culture, which should perhaps more properly be called a culture of cultures. Sicily's great cities are not palimpsests like such other Italian cities as Florence or Rome, where successive layers of culture build around, surpass, or even erase previous influences. In Sicily, on the contrary, the influences that have formed the island as it is today have never just existed side by side in cold, democratic respect, but rather have always blended into something new and original. In touring the island, it is easy to come upon massive Norman Romanesque churches beautifully harmonized with Arab ornamentation or classic Greek temples that have been transformed—without any loss of purpose or dignity—into splendid seventeenth-century Baroque masterpiece churches.

Without realizing it, one passes effortlessly from pink Byzantine domes to Arab honeycombed ceilings; from a villa with vintage first-century Roman mosaics to some of the best-preserved Doric temples in the world—without any sense of separation, until time itself falls away, and one is no longer in the fifth century or the twelfth, but in a place that is timeless, because it embodies all times. It is as if the seas surrounding Sicily have washed away the hard lines separating the various sand castles of its conquerors, and left behind a landscape strewn with values, customs, languages, and foods that is uniquely its own.

No single aspect of Sicilian culture better reflects Sicily's enduring ability to distill harmony out of diverse elements than its food. Sicilian cooking mingles Arab and Greek spices with Spanish and French sauces so that almost every popular dish is a living artifact of Sicily's long history. Apart from their composite origins, the recipes themselves are often blends of contrasting elements, like the sweet and sour taste of the ubiquitous eggplant *caponata*, or the hard and soft textures of fresh *cannoli*.

Sicily attracted Greek pirates as early as the fifth century B.C., and they brought with them the olive tree and the grapevine. When the Romans took over, they brought wheat, corn, and other grains, and turned Sicily's fertile soil into "the Granary of the Roman Empire." Soon after, the Sicilians started baking bread, and the island still produces some of the best breads in Italy.

The Arabs took Sicily in the ninth century and set up an emirate in Palermo with 300,000 inhabitants. It is hard to imagine now that they have all disappeared, but at one time Palermo had over 400 mosques within its precincts. The Arabs contributed rice, and the citrus groves and date palms that give Sicily its tropical appearance.

But most important of all, the Arabs brought their spices (saffron, cinnamon, cloves, sesame) and nuts, like the pistachios in one of Sicily's most popular desserts—*cassata siciliana*. This super-sweet confection consists of alternating layers of sponge cake and a filling made with ricotta cheese, cinnamon, and

chocolate custard. The whole is then covered with a pistachio-flavored glaze and elaborately decorated with flowers made from candied plums, figs, cherries, etc.

The Arabs also started the tuna and swordfish hunts which are still a major industry in Sicily. The *mattanza*, or tuna hunt, along the west coast near the island of Favignana attracted crowds of nobility in the eighteenth century, especially for the harpooning that followed the hauling in of the nets. It is still a thrilling, if somewhat bloody, spectacle.

The classic example of Arab-Sicilian culinary rapprochement is couscous, or *cuscus* in Sicilian (recipe page 243). *Cuscus* is steamed semolina; it is best sampled in Trapani where it is served with fish in summer and meat in winter. The flavor of this very simple dish depends entirely on the richness of the broth in which the semolina is steamed. *Cuscus* is prepared in a two-leveled pan called a *cuscusiera* where the steam from the broth below simmers and cooks the semolina above. When it is cooked, almost anything can be added to the semolina (mussels, lamb, shrimp, or vegetables) to form a hearty stew.

Many historians claim that it was the Arabs (and not Marco Polo) who brought pasta to Italy, and specifically to Sicily. Whether this is true or not, many pasta dishes in Sicily are definitely Arab-influenced. The most famous is probably *pasta con le sarde*, a sweet-and-sour blend of sardines, wild fennel, sultanas, pine nuts, and tomato sauce (recipe page 239). Nothing I know better represents the blend of contrasts that underlies Sicilian culture than *pasta con le sarde*, which incorporates the fish from Sicily's abundant waters, the raisins and nuts of its Arab past, the tomato and pasta of its more recent history, and the beard of the fennel plant that grows wild in the crevices of its ancient Greek temples like those at Segesta and Selinunte.

Other Arab-influenced dishes include *torrone*, nougat candy made with honey, sesame seeds, and almonds, and marzipan. Almond trees which grow all over the island (but are never more beautiful than those that blossom in early spring among the golden temples of Agrigento) are the source of the famous Sicilian marzipan (dipped in chocolate!) that you can see in the windows of shops along the Corso in Taormina. Here you can buy little straw baskets of marzipan shaped like rabbits or lambs, or like the fruits and vegetables that are typical of Sicily, such as *tarocchi* (blood oranges) or the ubiquitous *fico d'India* (prickly pear) which grows along the slopes of Taormina, fuschia-colored on the outside and a violent chartreuse inside.

The Spanish, who ruled Sicily from the fifteenth to the seventeenth centuries, brought the tomato from the New World, and this gave birth to a number of pasta dishes garnished with tomato sauce. *Pasta alla Norma* is named after the heroine of Vincenzo Bellini's opera of the same name. Bellini was born in Catania, where tomatoes thrive in the lava-rich soil on the slopes of Mount Etna. *Pasta alla Norma* is short pasta in an eggplant and tomato sauce, garnished with basil leaves and grated dry ricotta cheese.

Two young children in a Sicilian church vestry in 1957.

OPPOSITE
At Terra Rossa, a small colony run by the Martorana family near Taormina, a selection of Sicilian sweets: marzipan (pasta reale) shaped into fruits; a cassata cake; an almond cake; and little marzi-pan cookies made by nuns in the Santo Spirito monastery in Agrigento.

It was under Frederick II, the Holy Roman Emperor buried in the Palermo cathedral whose court was a bastion of high culture, that class distinctions became so entrenched in Sicily as to include what people ate. Two separate traditions of high and low cuisine persist on the island even today. The high cuisine is perhaps best represented by the *monzù* cooking, with its origins in the Kingdom of the Two Sicilies, when Sicily was joined to Naples by the Pope under the French house of Anjou, and Gallic flavors were introduced. The real advent of the *monzù* (from the French *monsieur*), however, occurred in the eighteenth and nineteenth centuries, when an elegant court cuisine was created by the *monsieurs,* the French chefs employed by the Bourbon nobility.

A classic example of this French influence is the Sicilian meat roll known as *farsumagru,* an adaptation of a French *roulé. Farsumagru* (or *falsomagro*) means literally "false lean," because what appears from the outside to be a simple meat roll is really a kind of roast cornucopia, bulging with ground veal, cheese, *prosciutto*, peas, salami, and hard-boiled eggs—everything that would impress the nobility, and that common people could never afford.

The Sicilian low cuisine can be found in Palermo's popular street food. During lunchtime, the labyrinthian side streets and tiny alleyways that make up the Vucciria market are full of tempting aromas. Office workers, businessmen, and secretaries from the nearby ministries form circles around vendors offering a variety of hot, spicy dishes—a kind of Italian fast food—which are served on buns or sometimes simply on a piece of butcher paper. Some encircle the big cast-iron pots of bubbling hot oil where the *frittella* or *frittedda* (a kind of Sicilian tempura) is being fried up; others yell out orders for *guasteddi* (fresh buns filled with piping-hot ribbons of calf's spleen, ricotta cheese, strands of goat's cheese, and a hot tomato sauce); still others want just a paper cone filled with *panelle* (chickpea flour fritters) or one or two *arancini* (deep-fried breaded rice balls filled with meat and cheese, recipe page 244). On the way back to work they will stop at a bar for coffee and a *cannolo*, the famous wafer "canals," which for my money are never better than in Palermo, where the fresh ricotta filling is always light and silky smooth, and never overpowers the hint of fennel seeds in the wafers.

Modern Sicily is still a land of contrasts. The traditional graciousness and nobility of the Sicilian people exist side by side with the atrocities and destructive presence of the Mafia. Alongside some of the most exquisite architecture the world has ever known, there is growing up some of the worst speculation in Europe. In recent years the island, like much of the Mediterranean coast, has seen a boom in popular tourism and a surge in seaside condominium development that has only recently begun to be checked. Moreover, the chic boutiques that sell the handsome lace and handmade linen in jet-set resort towns like Taormina often mask the poverty in which these wares are produced in towns like Enna and Caltanissetta.

In Homer's *Odyssey*, Sicily represented the last frontier—the border separating civilization from the Unknown—yet the region eventually became the center of the known world under the Normans. Across from Sicily's northeast coast, where Homer tells us Ulysses encountered one of the most ferocious challenges of his odyssey—the perilous rocks and terrible whirlpools of Scylla and Charybdis—the great *traghetti*, or ferryboats, still traverse the same waters shuttling cars, trains, and people from Sicily to the mainland.

OPPOSITE▶

A simple peasant meal of broad beans, pecorino cheese, corona *bread, and wine at Terra Rossa, near Taormina in Sicily.*

This trip is one of the great adventure rides of the real world. Whenever I take it, I always remain on deck and watch from the rear as the propellers churn these waters, once so fraught with danger and mystery, into translucent pools of gray-green alabaster. At night, it is the trail of white foam the propellers give off that I never tire of watching, under a sky that darkens with such gradual precision, it seems as though one of Ulysses' ancient gods was slowly emptying a bottle of ink into the enormous fish tank of the sky.

And when there is a full moon, and the *arancino* in my hand is still warm, I know that eventually a steel bridge will replace this ocean adventure, and Ulysses will recede even further into history. But I try to put this dour thought aside and, giving free rein to my imagination, I muse that if the captain of the ferryboat were Charon and the churning water below, the river Styx, how sweet eternity would be.

On the island of Sardinia, eligible men used to choose their wives, not for their beauty or their intelligence, but for their ability to bake bread. Even today, breadmaking among the Sardinians, who eat more of it than they do pasta, is almost a religious rite, and a woman who knows how to bake bread is still considered a woman of strong character and unusual competence.

Even though Sardinia is a patchwork of cultures, dialects, and customs, grain deities have persisted in its almost two-thousand-year history, and their influence is still felt in traditions, both religious and secular, in which bread is a dominant feature. On feast days and festivals, special *pani artistici* (artistic breads) are prepared that exemplify the imagination and ingenuity of *le donne sarde*, the Sardinian women. Some variety of these artistic breads appears in every Sardinian home at Christmas and Easter and on important saints' days; others are commissioned by friends for their weddings, baptisms, and other celebrations. The preparation often takes several days. After the dough is prepared from the abundant Sardinian durum (hard) wheat, it is cut into fantastic shapes or molded into intricate patterns (garlands, animals, coats-of-arms), sometimes incorporating whole eggs, apples, or oranges. Great pride is taken in these creations, as in any work of art.

The reason so much importance is given to bread in Sardinian culture probably stems from the fact that for every Sardinian on the island, there are at least two sheep. As a result, sheep or goat herding is the principal profession, and bread, which keeps well, can be carried up into high pastures, and needs no further preparation, is the perfect shepherd's food.

The Sardinian shepherd still dresses in the sheepskins and stocking cap of his ancestors, and lives much as they did, overseeing his roving flocks and moving with them when the grass is exhausted. To complement this pattern, the Sardinian women have developed *pane carasau*, a flatbread so light and thin that

◂ OPPOSITE
Fields near Castelvetrano in Sicily.   *Man on a mule near Laconi in Sardinia.*

it has been nicknamed *carta di musica*, or sheet music bread. It is the bread that the Sardinian shepherd has been eating for centuries, and is closer to the unleavened breads found in the Middle East or India than to the bread of other parts of Italy.

Carta di musica is baked in straw-fired ovens outside the house. The loaves are manipulated in the oven by means of iron *palette*, or paddles, that have long wooden handles. The thin, thin sheets of bread are almost transparent when they come out of the oven in crisp toasted leaves, which are piled one on top of the other, like the pages of some ancient manuscript, to cool. The best *carta di musica* is difficult to make: it must never be burnt, but at the same time, it must develop tiny characteristic bubbles or cracks on its surface, which make the bread look appetizing as well as taste good.

Pane carasau is the perfect light accompaniment to the island's principal meat dishes—roast suckling pig garnished with rosemary, or lamb savored with heather. But it can also be eaten alone, spread with *pecorino* (sheep's milk) cheese, then folded and served warm or brushed with olive oil, sprinkled with rosemary, and reheated. Sardinian *pecorino* is not one cheese but many that have been worked by the shepherds to produce various textures from creamy to crunchy, depending on the aging. The crust is a dark golden yellow and the inside varies from straw yellow to snow white.

Pane frattau, a variation of *carta di musica*, is a meal in itself. It is made from the simplest of ingredients and perfectly represents the *cucina povera*, the unpretentious common-man's cooking that is at the heart of Sardinian cuisine. First, three or four layers of flat round shepherd's bread are covered with grated *pecorino* cheese, then a bit of beef broth (*brodo*) or tomato sauce is added, and finally a fried egg is slipped into the center of the top layer. *Pane frattau* is the perfect symbol of rocky, crusty, sunny Sardinia. Its translucency recalls the clear blue waters; the white and yellow of the egg represent the abundant sunshine; and the crisp, crunchy surface reminds one of the Sardinian character—which can be hard to penetrate at first, but is easily broken by a smile or a joke.

Thanks to the ruggedness and remoteness of much of Sardinia, the old customs and traditions are still very much alive. Moreover, the Sardinian language has developed independently from the Italian spoken on the mainland, and preserves certain archaic features, which give it a lilting, softly sibilant charm. *Ravioli*, for example, are called *purlurgiones*, or *culingiones* (recipe page 236); in Sardo *gnocchi* are known as *malloreddus*.

Outside the tourist areas the *cucina povera* is still the basis of all Sardinian cooking and maintains its character as a simple, nutritious diet of meats roasted with herbs on an open fire, vegetables prepared with olive oil, sheep or goat cheese, and sweets made with honey and nuts. There is even the poor man's caviar—

Carta di musica, *"sheet music bread," at the Albergo Sacchi near Nuoro in Sardinia.*

OPPOSITE▶
Pane frattau, *made with* carta di musica, *tomato sauce, egg, and cheese, at the Albergo Sacchi.*

la bottarga, made from tuna or mullet roe. The eggs are extracted immediately after the fish is captured, when the ovarial sack is still intact; they are then salted, dried, and pressed into a block. The best Sardinian *bottarga* comes from the mullet that inhabit the Cabras lagoon. It is eaten either as an antipasto, sliced thin on pieces of bread garnished with olive oil or lemon, or it is grated abundantly on top of hot spaghetti.

A legend says that despite the presence of numerous prehistoric stone structures—the famous *nuraghi*—all over the island, Sardinia was created late in time from a piece of land the gods did not know what to do with when they had finished making the world. What they tossed into the Mediterranean turned into a sumptuous feast made from leftovers. Long, pearly white sand beaches stretch out near Cagliari, the capital and commercial port on the island's southern coast; on the northern coast, the winds coming down from France across Corsica have carved out amazing rock formations. Sardinia's inland is mountainous, but cut through with dramatic gorges and rivers. Some of the mountains shelter spectacular grottoes like those at Capo Caccia and Cala Gonone. From Cagliari northwest to Oristano on the west coast extends the Campidano, a fertile plain that ends on the Sinis peninsula, where pink flamingos haunt shallow lagoons and mysterious-looking salt mines create desert-like dunes.

But the Sardinian paradise of fine beaches and clear waters is slowly changing, particularly as a result of tourism, which is booming with the building of hotel complexes, the most spectacular of which are the luxury developments on the Costa Smeralda (the Emerald Coast), built by the Aga Khan on a strip of northeast coastline. While it is true that these complexes have little in common with the traditional values represented by the Sardinian bread-baking and sheepherding culture, they have at the same time brought fame, alternative employment, and considerable fortune to what were previously abandoned beaches.

The transition from a traditional sheepherding economy to a tourist economy will not be easy, and will inevitably disturb the uniqueness of this leftover bit of paradise, where once upon a time people took pride in simple things, praised each other for their common sense, and told their sons that a woman who had the skill to bake bread as thin as paper had to be good of heart.

Louis Inturrisi

◄ OPPOSITE
Sallasicce *(a kind of sausage),* agnello *(lamb), and* maialino *(piglet), roasting on spits at the Albergo Sacchi on Monte Ortobene near Nuoro in Sardinia.*

An antipasto called grive *made of* tordi *(thrushes), boiled and served cold with myrtle and salt at the Ristorante Sa Cardiga e su Schironi in Cagliari, the capital of Sardinia.*

Raw ingredients for frittedda, *Sicilian dialect for* minestra di primavera, *at Terra Rossa (recipe right, using spring onions instead of the yellow onions pictured here).*

This dish is made for Saint Joseph's Day, March 19, a very important spring holiday in Italy. Frittedda *can be served as a first course, or as a sauce for pasta. One Palermo version is made with a sweet-and-sour sauce; in Taormina, tops of wild fennel are added.*

Frittedda   Braised Spring Vegetables

From Mrs. Martorana of Terra Rossa, Taormina

Serves 6

2 pounds fresh green peas
2 pounds fresh broad beans
6 fresh artichokes, or 6 thinly sliced
  canned or frozen artichoke hearts
2 tablespoons fresh lemon juice,
  plus extra for garnish

1 pound spring onions, bulbs
  chopped, green tops chopped
  and used for garnish
6 tablespoons olive oil
Salt and pepper to taste
Butter for garnish to taste (optional)

Shell the peas and broad beans. To prepare the fresh artichokes, remove all their outer leaves by snapping them off above the bottom white part of the leaf. When you have reached the inner "cone," where the leaves are green only at the top 1 inch, cut that top off. Then go inside the choke with a rounded knife or sharp-edged spoon to cut out the inner leaves and the little hairs (the "beard") beneath them. Pare away some more of the green outer part of the leaves at the base of each artichoke, and cut off the stems. Dribble lemon juice over the prepared artichokes as you complete the others, to keep them from going brown. Slice the artichokes thin vertically, and soak the pieces in water and the lemon juice.

Sauté the chopped spring onion bulbs with the olive oil in a large frying pan, then add the drained artichoke hearts, season with salt and pepper, and cook gently over medium heat until the artichokes are half done. The timing will depend on the tenderness of the artichokes, and the type used; add up to ¼ cup water if necessary. Then add the broad beans and the peas, pour in ½ cup water, cover, and cook, stirring occasionally, for 10 to 15 minutes, until the vegetables are tender.

When the vegetables are ready to serve, adjust seasoning to taste. You can also add some fresh lemon juice and butter, if desired. Garnish with chopped spring onion tops and serve.   *(Photographs above left and opposite page)*

A man plowing his vineyard in Ummari in Sicily.

OPPOSITE ▶
Ingredients for frittedda *ready to assemble at Terra Rossa (recipe above).*

Culingiones, *the most common Sardinian* ravioli, *decoratively shaped and laid on lemon leaves at the Ristorante Su Meriagu in Cagliari (recipe right).*

Because of the prevalence of bread on the island, there are but three main local pasta dishes on Sardinia: malloreddus, *little dumplings, flavored with saffron and served with spicy tomato sauce and* pecorino *cheese;* ciciones, *tiny dumplings flavored with saffron and dressed with roast juices or tomato sauce; and the* culingiones *that follow.*

Culingiones   Sardinian Ravioli

From the Laconi Sisters of the Ristorante Su Meriagu, Cagliari

Serves 4

The pasta:
2½ cups durum wheat flour
4 eggs
Pinch of salt

The filling:
⅔ pound fresh spinach
1 tablespoon salt
2 tablespoons butter
3 eggs
1 tablespoon flour

2 cups freshly grated Sardinian
    pecorino cheese, or *pecorino*
    romano cheese
1 tablespoon pepper
¼ teaspoon powdered saffron
¼ teaspoon grated nutmeg

The topping:
Tomato sauce (recipe page 218)
⅓ cup rinsed and chopped fresh
    basil leaves
½ cup freshly grated *pecorino* cheese

Make the pasta using the ingredients listed here according to the directions on page 247. Let the dough rest in a dishcloth for about 15 minutes.

To make the filling, put 1 inch of water in a large pot. Wash the spinach and remove the stems. When the water boils, add the salt and cook the spinach, covered, for 2 minutes, stirring once. Then drain, cool, squeeze dry, and chop. Sauté the spinach lightly in a pan with the butter; then mix the spinach in a bowl with the rest of the ingredients for the filling.

Prepare the pasta dough to make the *culingiones* following the directions for stuffed pasta on page 247; each finished *ravioli* should be about 2 inches long, to allow enough pasta for folding. Put heaping tablespoons of the filling on the dough lengths, then fold the dough over to cover the filling, seal the edges together, and cut the *culingiones* using a pastry cutter. (In Sardinia, traditional *culingiones* are made in a half-moon shape by cutting the pasta in 3-inch rounds, placing the filling on the round, folding over the round, and pinching at the edges.)

Cook the *culingiones* in plenty of boiling salted water for 10 minutes. Drain, and serve dressed with fresh tomato sauce, chopped basil, and grated *pecorino* cheese.   *(Photograph above left)*

1. *Mother and child on a farm in Ummari in Sicily.*

2. *Bread and* pecorino *cheese in Sardinia.*

3. *Beef offal and innards hanging in the street in Mazara del Vallo south of Marsala in Sicily.*

4. *An array of favorite Sardinian flavors: a plate of myrtle leaves, dried tomatoes and chiles, and salt at the Ristorante Su Meriagu in Cagliari.*

5. *A jar of Sicilian olives preserved in vinegar and herbs at the market in Taormina.*

6. *Chickens and rabbits at the market in Licata, on the southern coast of Sicily.*

7. *A serving of eels cooked with laurel leaves and salt at the Ristorante Sa Cardiga e su Schironi near Cagliari in Sardinia.*

8. *Another version of* culingiones *at the Albergo Sacchi on Monte Ortobene, Sardinia (similar recipe above).*

9. *A young Sicilian girl photographed in a hill town near Taormina in 1957.*

1

2

3

4

5

6

7

8

9

Pasta con le Sarde   Pasta with Sardines

From Mrs. Martorana of Terra Rossa, Taormina

Serves 4

1 fennel bulb with greens
1 cup peeled and chopped onion
6 tablespoons olive oil
1 tablespoon tomato paste
¼ cup raisins, soaked in warm water
¼ cup pine nuts
10 fresh sardines, cleaned, boned,
   heads removed (you can use
   canned sardines, if necessary,
   rinsed and drained)

Salt and pepper to taste
4 anchovy fillets packed in oil
¾ pound dried macaroni
   or spaghetti

Cook the fennel in plenty of boiling salted water for about 10 minutes, until tender. Drain the fennel water into another large pot, saving for later use. Pat the fennel dry, and chop to yield about 2 cups.

In a large saucepan, sauté the onion in 4 tablespoons olive oil, then add the tomato paste diluted with ¼ cup of the fennel cooking water, the drained raisins, and the pine nuts. Simmer for about 5 minutes. Open the sardines out flat, and add them to the other simmering ingredients. After another 10 minutes, add the chopped fennel. Season with salt and pepper, cover, and cook over moderate heat for about 5 minutes, turning the fish from time to time until they are cooked.

Sauté the anchovies in a small saucepan over low heat with the remaining 2 tablespoons of olive oil until they disintegrate, and then add them with their oil to the sardine mixture.

Boil the reserved water used for the fennel, adding more water if needed, and cook the pasta until *al dente*. Drain and dress with the sauce, arrange the sardines on the pasta, and serve.

(Photographs above right and opposite page)

Pasta con le sarde ready to eat at Terra Rossa (recipe left). This method of sprinkling breadcrumbs instead of cheese over the food was traditionally a way for the poor to add texture and flavor to their dishes.

A shepherd with his flock on the beach near Licata in Sicily.

◄ OPPOSITE
The ingredients for pasta con le sarde at Terra Rossa, near Taormina in Sicily (recipe above).

Marie-Louise Martorana's ditali con cavolfiore *at Terra Rossa (recipe right).*

OPPOSITE PAGE▶
Ingredients for Marie-Louise Martorana's ditali con cavolfiore *at Terra Rossa near Taormina in Sicily.*

Two women arguing in a narrow street near the harbor in Licata, on the southern coast of Sicily.

Ditali con Broccoli o Cavolfiore

Ditali Pasta with Broccoli or Cauliflower

From Mrs. Martorana of Terra Rossa, Taormina

Serves 4

2 stalks broccoli, or 1 medium
cauliflower, washed and trimmed
into florets to yield about 5 cups
5 tablespoons olive oil
1 cup peeled and finely chopped
onion
⅛ teaspoon powdered saffron,
dissolved in 1 tablespoon water
6 anchovy fillets packed in oil

½ cup raisins, soaked in warm water
⅓ cup pine nuts, toasted in the oven
1½ pounds *ditali* pasta, or any short
macaroni
½ cup freshly grated mature
Sardinian *pecorino* cheese,
or *pecorino romano* cheese
⅓ cup rinsed and chopped fresh
basil leaves

Cook the broccoli or cauliflower florets in plenty of boiling salted water until *al dente*. Drain the water into another large pot, saving for later use.

Pour 3 tablespoons of olive oil into a large frying pan and sauté the chopped onion over low heat; then add the saffron. Add the broccoli or cauliflower florets, and cover.

Boil the water left over from the vegetables. At the same time, cook the anchovies in a small pan in the remaining 2 tablespoons of olive oil until they disintegrate. Add them to the broccoli or cauliflower mixture, along with the drained raisins and toasted pine nuts. Stir the sauce, cook for 5 minutes, then remove from the heat.

Meanwhile, cook the pasta in the boiling vegetable water until *al dente*, then drain and mix with the vegetables in a large serving bowl. Serve with the grated cheese and chopped basil on top.
(Photographs above left and opposite page)

Pasta is the main dish of Southern Italian cooking. In the past and even today it is a piatto unico, *a full meal, when served with various ingredients like vegetables, fish, meat, eggs, or cheese. Here is a very simple example from Terra Rossa, a small colony near Taormina run by the Martorana family.*

Pasta con Aglio   Pasta with Garlic

From Mrs. Martorana of Terra Rossa, Taormina

Serves 4

½ cup peeled and chopped almonds
6 cloves garlic, peeled
6 fresh ripe plum tomatoes, peeled
¾ cup rinsed and coarsely chopped
fresh basil leaves

Salt and pepper to taste
¼ cup olive oil
1¼ pounds dried macaroni

Toast the almonds in a baking pan in a 250° oven, keeping an eye on them so they do not burn. Then pound the garlic, tomatoes, almonds, and basil together in a large mortar, or put them through a blender. Season with salt and pepper, add the olive oil, and mash everything together well. (If using a blender, mix in the olive oil by hand using a wooden spoon.)

Cook the macaroni in plenty of boiling salted water. When done, drain it, dress it with the sauce, and serve.

Cuscus con Pesce Fish Couscous

From Mr. Catalano of the Hotel Moderno, Erice

Serves 4

Aromatics (5 peppercorns, 2 bay leaves, ¼ teaspoon cinnamon, 1 teaspoon salt, 1 peeled clove garlic)
One 10-ounce box instant couscous
1 cup peeled and chopped onion
6 tablespoons extra virgin olive oil
1 tablespoon butter
Salt and pepper to taste
3 teaspoons peeled and finely chopped garlic
1 cup peeled and finely chopped almonds, toasted in the oven
2 cups seeded and chopped fresh tomatoes
1 teaspoon seeded and finely chopped serrano chile pepper
2 pounds assorted fish fillets (codfish, snapper, sole, and the like)
3 tablespoons chopped parsley
1 cup white wine

Put the aromatics in 2 cups water in the bottom of a double boiler, and put the water on to boil. Place the couscous in a strainer that will fit over the pot. Run cold water over the couscous, mixing the grains with your hands to ensure even moistening. Drain, then spread the couscous on a sheet pan and let it rest for 10 minutes. In a medium-sized pan sauté the chopped onion in 4 tablespoons olive oil until translucent.

Take the couscous from the pan, and breaking up any lumps, put the couscous into the strainer, and set it over the boiling water. Add the onion and oil to the couscous with the butter, salt, and pepper, and stir. Let it steam for about 15 minutes, as tightly covered as possible, stirring a few times to break up any lumps. Then remove from heat and keep covered.

Meanwhile, in a large pot sauté the garlic in 2 tablespoons olive oil with the almonds and tomatoes. Season with salt and pepper, and add the chile pepper. Cook for about 10 minutes, then add the fish in pieces, placing the most delicate kinds at the top, and 2 tablespoons parsley. Add the white wine and let the soup simmer for a few minutes, then cover and cook for about 20 minutes, adding up to ½ cup water if needed for moisture.

When the fish soup is ready, place the couscous in a large heated bowl, ladle the soup around it, and garnish with 1 tablespoon parsley.

Spaghetti coi Granchi Spaghetti with Crab Sauce

From the Ristorante Sa Cardiga e su Schironi, Cagliari

Serves 4

1 teaspoon peeled and finely chopped garlic
1 teaspoon seeded and finely chopped serrano chile pepper
½ cup plus 2 tablespoons olive oil
1 pound crab meat, broken in pieces
to yield 2 cups
1 cup seeded and coarsely chopped fresh tomatoes
¼ teaspoon salt
2 teaspoons chopped parsley
1 pound spaghetti or *linguine*

Heat the garlic and chile pepper in a frying pan with ½ cup of the olive oil. Add the crab in pieces, then the tomatoes. Simmer until all the water has evaporated; then add the salt and parsley.

Cook the pasta in plenty of boiling salted water until it is *al dente*. Drain, dress with the crab sauce and the remaining olive oil, and serve. *(Photograph right)*

A fisherman with his net in Licata on the southern coast of Sicily.

◄ OPPOSITE PAGE
Shellfish in baskets at the Ristorante Sa Cardiga e su Schironi in Cagliari in Sardinia. Clockwise from top left: canno-licchi *(razor clams),* cozze *(mussels),* granchetti *(baby crabs),* arselle *(baby clams),* fasolari *(pink clams),* tartufi di mare *(venus clams), and* ostriche *(oysters).*

Spaghetti coi granchi *ready to be served at the Ristorante Sa Cardiga e su Schironi (recipe left).*

Oranges and lemons for sale on a chair in Calatafimi, Sicily.

Arancini di Riso   "Little Orange" Rice Balls

From Mrs. Martorana of Terra Rossa, Taormina

Serves 6

Salt	½ pound lean ground beef
2 cups Arborio rice	¼ cup raisins
¼ cup olive oil	½ cup dry white wine
2 tablespoons tomato sauce	½ cup *primo sale* or fontina cheese
¼ cup grated *caciocavallo*	cubes (¼-inch dice)
or *provolone* cheese	¼ cup *mortadella* cubes
Pepper	(¼-inch dice)
¼ cup pine nuts	1 cup flour
½ cup peeled and finely chopped	2 eggs, beaten
onion	1 cup plain dried breadcrumbs
2 tablespoons tomato paste	Vegetable oil for frying

Boil 3 quarts of water in a large saucepan, add 2 tablespoons of salt, and the rice. Return to a boil, reduce heat, and simmer until rice is *al dente*, about 20 minutes. Drain the rice, then mix it in a bowl with 3 tablespoons olive oil, the tomato sauce, the grated *caciocavallo* cheese, and salt and pepper to taste. Spread the rice out on a sheet pan and leave to cool for 2 hours.

About ½ hour before the rice is cool, toast the pine nuts in a baking pan in a 250° oven, keeping an eye on them so they do not burn. Sauté the onion in 1 tablespoon olive oil in a saucepan, add the tomato paste, stir, and cook for 2 minutes. Next add the ground beef, raisins, pine nuts, and wine, stir, and cook for about 20 minutes, seasoning with 2 teaspoons salt and 1 teaspoon pepper. Then remove the pan from the heat, and add the *primo sale* cheese and the *mortadella*. Thoroughly mix these ingredients with the rice in a large bowl. Add another 2 teaspoons of salt and 1 teaspoon of pepper.

Make round, smooth balls with the mixture, the size of small oranges (for best results, make the balls somewhat oval, like an egg). Roll the balls first in flour, then in egg, and finally in the breadcrumbs. Deep-fry them in plenty of hot oil over medium heat until golden brown. Drain and serve.

Insalata di Arancie   Orange Salad

From Mrs. Martorana of Terra Rossa, Taormina

Serves 4

5 seedless, juicy oranges	1 tablespoon finely chopped fennel
¼ cup olive oil	bulb (optional)
Salt to taste	1 tablespoon chopped parsley
1 small red onion	(optional)

Peel the oranges, removing as much of the white inner pith as possible, and then slice the oranges in thin rounds. Put them on a large serving plate, sprinkle them with the olive oil, and season with salt. Peel the onion and cut it in thin rings; soak the rings in ice water if the onion flavor is too strong.

Tilt the serving plate, and with a large spoon scoop up the olive oil and juices to baste the oranges. Drain the onion slices and add them to the oranges. Baste so that more juice mingles with the oil; chopped fennel and parsley can also be added, to taste. Let the salad sit for half an hour or more to allow the flavors to blend, and serve.   *(Photograph opposite page)*

OPPOSITE PAGE ▶
The ingredients and finished result of insalata di arancie *at Terra Rossa (recipe right).*

Appendix

Each region, perhaps even each cook, in Italy devises an individual method for pasta, the country's most beloved and important food. Following is a very basic method for the preparation of pasta, which can be used on its own, or as a guideline for the other pasta recipes in the book.

Basic Egg Pasta

Proportions:

For 3 or 4 persons: 1½ cups flour, 2 eggs
For 5 or 6 persons: 2¼ cups flour, 3 eggs
For 7 or 8 persons: 3 cups flour, 4 eggs
(these proportions go further in stuffed pasta recipes)

See your recipe for any specific proportions of flour, eggs, or other ingredients required.

Place the flour on a pastry board or in a large mixing bowl. Make a well in the center of the flour, and crack the eggs into the well. Using a fork, beat the eggs, drawing the flour into the eggs a little at a time. If other ingredients are called for in the pasta recipe, they may be added at this time.

When the dough begins to hold together and the eggs are completely absorbed into the flour, it is ready to be kneaded. If you are using a bowl, move the dough to a flat work surface to knead. Flour your hands lightly.

Work the dough with your hands until it forms a ball. Discard any extra bits of flour or dough that have not been absorbed into the dough. Knead for 5 minutes by folding the dough toward you and then pressing it away from you with the heels of your hands, rotating the dough at quarter turns between each fold. You may have to add a little more flour to the dough and/or your hands during this time if the dough starts to stick. After you have finished kneading, and the dough is nice and smooth, wrap it in a clean, damp dishcloth and let it rest for 10 minutes. Divide the dough into 6 pieces.

For stuffed pasta:

If you are using a pasta machine, run each piece of dough through the machine, starting with the greatest thickness and moving down to the next smallest thickness each time. The second to last thickness will be right for making *ravioli, tortellini,* and other stuffed pastas.

Allow the dough to rest for about 15 minutes after you have rolled it out, or until it feels dry to the touch.

Place spoonsful of your filling about 2 inches apart in rows on 3 of the pasta sheets, or as directed in the recipe. Place the other 3 sheets of pasta over the first 3 and press down around the mounds of filling with your fingers to seal the packets. (You can brush the pasta areas to be sealed with a little beaten egg yolk or water to ensure a firm seal.) Finally, use a pastry wheel to cut the pasta around the filling mounds into individual *ravioli* squares. Let the *ravioli* sit for a few minutes, not touching, before cooking them in 8 to 10 quarts of boiling salted water for 3 to 4 minutes.

To make *tortellini,* cut the sheets of dough into 2-inch squares using a pastry cutter. Place small spoonsful of your filling on each square, moisten the edges, fold the dough over to make a triangle, and seal all around. Wrap the straight edge of the packet around your forefinger and press the ends together to make the *tortellini.* Proceed to cook as indicated above.

For *tagliatelle:*

If you are using a pasta machine, follow the directions for *ravioli,* but roll the dough out through the very last, thinnest setting. Allow the dough to rest for about 15 minutes after you have rolled it out, or until it feels dry to the touch. Roll each sheet of dough up, as for a jelly roll, and cut the rolls horizontally into ¼-inch strips, using a sharp knife (or leave the sheets of pasta flat and roll them through the wider cutting blades of the pasta machine). Unravel these strips and you will have your *tagliatelle.* Allow the strips to sit for about 10 minutes, not touching, on wax paper, and then cook them for a minute in 8 to 10 quarts of boiling, salted water.

If you are making the pasta by hand with a rolling pin, roll out the dough about ⅛ inch thick for stuffed pastas, and ⅟₁₆ inch thick for *tagliatelle.*

After you have kneaded the dough and let it rest in a dishcloth, divide it into 4 sections. Flatten out each section with your hand to an oblong about 1 inch thick, lightly sprinkle it with flour, and proceed to roll it out to the desired thickness with a heavy rolling pin, being very careful that the dough is not sticking to the work surface. Lift it gingerly and sprinkle flour under the dough if it starts to stick. When it is rolled out, allow the dough to rest for 15 minutes, and then proceed with the directions in your recipe, or the directions above.

Acknowledgments

In the introduction I mentioned some of the people who helped me put this book together, but more space is needed to acknowledge all the others.

First and foremost I must express my profound gratitude to a group of very creative people at the *London Sunday Times Magazine*. They made my work in this book possible in the first place, by commissioning me to do a nine-part series of articles on what they titled "The Taste of Italy." (This series followed an earlier project done with them, "The Taste of France.")

Under the constant direction of Michael Rand, the creative force and director of the magazine, and the indispensable Suzanne Hodgart, the *Times* did all the preliminary research needed to approach such a project, and supported me fully throughout the months of its realization.

They enlisted the talents of Claudia Roden, author of best-selling books on Middle Eastern and Mediterranean cookery, to write the texts for "The Taste of Italy." The series was soundly edited by Brenda Jones, and lavishly designed by Gilvrie Misstear.

The success of the series encouraged me to gather other photographic material for the book from at least three other trips in Italy—some done many years ago, and a last one done recently to fill in the gaps.

The whole project spanned a period of two years, including six months on the road in Italy, covering more than 30,000 miles. This could only have been accomplished with the essential support of Marilyn Costa as our interpreter, researcher, and guide, and Vicki Emmett as my photographic assistant. They both put up patiently with the erratic and temperamental behavior of this photographer!

No book project like this is ever done alone.

Back in the United States, with the dedicated help and constant advice of my representatives Peter Schub and Robert Bear, we enlisted the publishing experience of Nicholas Callaway to realize much more than just a "cookbook."

Over the next twelve months, with the help of everyone at Callaway Editions, I was led by the hand through the preparation of this book. Alexandra Arrowsmith's thoroughly methodical and analytical editing qualities separated the essential from the trivial in the text, recipes, and captions.

True Sims organized the production schedules, and Toshiya Masuda, assisted by Ivan Wong, Jr., rendered the whole project in layouts by coordinating my selection of photographs with the requirements of the text and production.

At the recommendation of Nicholas Callaway, I enlisted the talents of Bert Clarke as typographer. He taught me the balance and harmony of text and image on the page.

I must mention my gratitude to Charles Melcher, publisher at Callaway, who managed to soothe our feelings at times of frustration and turmoil. And a special "thank you" to Norma Spriggs, for patiently coordinating our efforts on this project at Schub & Bear.

We tried to list throughout the pages of this book the places and names of all the Italian people, chefs, cooks, and restaurant owners who contributed their help and hospitality. I trust I have not forgotten some unsung hero who put up with us.

After all the traveling through Italy I have learned two things: patience with Italian drivers!! and admiration for the professionalism of all the people involved in the art of growing, preparing, and serving food not only to their compatriots but also to the millions of us who come to appreciate their hospitality and their history.

With love I finally dedicate this book to my wife, Jeannette, who came along whenever possible to contribute her impeccable taste and her great appreciation of Italian art and history.

To our daughter, Babette, let this book be a tribute to her patience waiting for us while pursuing her medical studies in New York.

Robert Freson

About the Contributors

Writers   CAROL FIELD is the author of *The Hill Towns of Italy* (E. P. Dutton, 1983), *The Italian Baker* (Harper & Row, 1985), and *Celebrating Italy* (Morrow, 1990). She lives in San Francisco.

LESLIE FORBES is the illustrator and author of *A Table in Tuscany: Classic Recipes from the Heart of Italy* (paperback edition Chronicle Books, 1991) and, most recently, *Remarkable Feasts* (Simon & Schuster, 1991). She lives in London.

BARBARA GRIZZUTI HARRISON is the author of *Italian Days* (Weidenfeld & Nicolson, 1989). She has published in *Harper's Magazine* and *The Nation,* among numerous other periodicals, and was awarded the O'Henry Prize for Short Fiction in 1989.

LOUIS INTURRISI is a freelance writer on Italian food and culture living in Rome. He has been published in *Gourmet, HG,* and *The New York Times.*

BEATRICE MUZI is a sculptress and author born in Le Marche who founded and runs the Scuola Italiana del Greenwich Village in New York. She co-wrote *La Cucina Picena* (Padua: Muzzio, 1991), a survey of the indigenous peasant cooking of her native region, together with Allan Evans, a musicologist, who also collaborated on the essay in this book.

PAOLA PETTINI is a food historian who runs a cooking school in Bari. She served as an advisor to Robert Freson in Apulia, and also contributed several recipes to the book.

VITO QUARANTA is an Italian food connoisseur and a member of the Cordon Bleu Association. He lives in Verona and served as advisor to Robert Freson in Veneto.

NADIA STANCIOFF is the Director of Public Relations for Orient-Express Hotels worldwide, in London. Her writing has appeared often in *Gourmet* magazine, and she has lived in Umbria for sixteen years.

SAM TANENHAUS is a literary scholar and avid Italophile who has traveled all over and written about various aspects of Italy. He lives with his Italian-born wife in New York.

VANESSA SOMERS VREELAND is a British artist, Roman by adoption. Together with her husband, the U.S. Ambassador to Morocco, she is the co-author of the *Access* Guide to Rome, for which they won Rome's Silver Medal for Tourism.

Recipe researcher   MARILYN COSTA was born and educated in Sydney, Australia. She lives and works as a freelance consultant in Turin. A long love affair with Italian cuisine led to her contribution to the "Taste of Italy" series for the *London Sunday Times* in 1988, as researcher and photographic coordinator.

Recipe tester   JOHANNA SEMPLE began her culinary career in Italy under the tutelage of Fabio Benedetto Picci in Florence. After two years she returned to America to work with Marcella Hazan at restaurants in Atlanta and Dallas. She is now a sous-chef at Mustard's Grill in the Napa Valley, northern California.

Index

This book was produced by Callaway Editions, under the direction of Nicholas Callaway and Charles Melcher. Alexandra Arrowsmith was editor, with assistance from Jin Park. True Sims was director of production, assisted by Ivan Wong, Jr. The text was copyedited and proofread by Barbara Bergeron, Jane Mollman, Andrea Belloli, and Alessandra Visconti (who also translated two essays for the book). Martha Lazar and José Rodriguez assisted in all aspects of production.

Susan Friedland was the editor for the book at HarperCollins. Johanna Semple, Peter Hall, and Charlene Nicholson of Mustard's Grill in Napa Valley, California, tested the recipes and adapted them for American kitchens.

Bert Clarke was the designer for the book. Toshiya Masuda set and generated the type, using QuarkXPress® 3.1 on a Macintosh™ IIci with a 21-inch Radius™ black-and-white monitor. The text typeface is Adobe Minion™. The display type is Monotype Bembo®. The type was output by The Sarabande Press, New York. The maps were drawn by T. R. Lundquist, New York, using Adobe Illustrator® on a Macintosh™ IIci.

Separations for the book were laser-scanned with a 150-line screen by Nissha Printing Company, Kyoto, Japan. Hiroyuki Nakao coordinated production for Nissha. The book was printed and bound by Sung In Printing, Seoul, Korea, under the supervision of Wayne Turner and Toshiya Masuda.